D1371048

The Mirage of
Global Markets

In an increasingly competitive world, it is quality
of thinking that gives an edge—an idea that opens new
doors, a technique that solves a problem, or an insight
that simply helps make sense of it all.

We work with leading authors in the various arenas
of business and finance to bring cutting-edge thinking
and best learning practice to a global market.

It is our goal to create world-class print publications
and electronic products that give readers
knowledge and understanding which can then be
applied, whether studying or at work.

To find out more about our business
products, you can visit us at www.ft-ph.com

The Mirage of
Global Markets

How Globalizing Companies
Can Succeed
as Markets Localize

David Arnold

FT Prentice Hall
FINANCIAL TIMES

An Imprint of PEARSON EDUCATION
Upper Saddle River, NJ • New York • London • San Francisco • Toronto • Sydney
Tokyo • Singapore • Hong Kong • Cape Town • Madrid
Paris • Milan • Munich • Amsterdam

www.ft-ph.com

Library of Congress Cataloging-in-Publication Data

A CIP record of this book can be obtained from the Library of Congress.

Production Supervisor: *Faye Gemmellaro*
Manufacturing Buyer: *Maura Zaldivar*
Cover Design Director: *Jerry Votta*
Interior Design: *Gail Cocker-Bogusz*
VP, Editor-in-Chief: *Tim Moore*
Editorial Assistant: *Richard Winkler*
Developmental Editor: *Russ Hall*
Marketing Manager: *John Pierce*

© 2004 Pearson Education, Inc.
Publishing as Financial Times Prentice Hall
Upper Saddle River, New Jersey 07458

Financial Times Prentice Hall offers excellent discounts on this book when ordered in quantity for bulk purchases or special sales. For more information, please contact: U.S. Corporate and Government Sales, 1-800-382-3419, corpsales@pearsontechgroup.com. For sales outside of the United States, please contact: International Sales, 1-317-581-3793, international@pearsontechgroup.com.

Company and product names mentioned herein are the trademarks or registered trademarks of their respective owners.

All rights reserved. No part of this book may be reproduced, in any form or by any means, without permission in writing from the publisher.

Printed in the United States of America

Second Printing

ISBN 0-13-047066-X

Pearson Education Ltd.
Pearson Education Australia Pty., Limited
Pearson Education Singapore, Pte. Ltd.
Pearson Education North Asia Ltd.
Pearson Education Canada, Ltd.
Pearson Educación de Mexico, S.A. de C.V.
Pearson Education—Japan
Pearson Education Malaysia, Pte. Ltd.

For Megan, Kate, and Thomas

FINANCIAL TIMES PRENTICE HALL BOOKS

For more information, please go to www.ft-ph.com

Business and Technology

Sarv Devaraj and Rajiv Kohli

> *The IT Payoff: Measuring the Business Value of Information Technology Investments*

Nicholas D. Evans

> *Business Innovation and Disruptive Technology: Harnessing the Power of Breakthrough Technology...for Competitive Advantage*

Nicholas D. Evans

> *Consumer Gadgets: 50 Ways to Have Fun and Simplify Your Life with Today's Technology...and Tomorrow's*

Faisal Hoque

> *The Alignment Effect: How to Get Real Business Value Out of Technology*

Economics

David Dranove

> *What's Your Life Worth? Health Care Rationing...Who Lives? Who Dies? Who Decides?*

John C. Edmunds

> *Brave New Wealthy World: Winning the Struggle for World Prosperity*

Jonathan Wight

> *Saving Adam Smith: A Tale of Wealth, Transformation, and Virtue*

Entrepreneurship

Oren Fuerst and Uri Geiger

> *From Concept to Wall Street: A Complete Guide to Entrepreneurship and Venture Capital*

David Gladstone and Laura Gladstone

> *Venture Capital Handbook: An Entrepreneur's Guide to Raising Venture Capital, Revised and Updated*

Erica Orloff and Kathy Levinson, Ph.D.

> *The 60-Second Commute: A Guide to Your 24/7 Home Office Life*

Jeff Saperstein and Daniel Rouach

> *Creating Regional Wealth in the Innovation Economy: Models, Perspectives, and Best Practices*

Finance

Aswath Damodaran
  The Dark Side of Valuation: Valuing Old Tech, New Tech, and New Economy Companies

Kenneth R. Ferris and Barbara S. Pécherot Petitt
  Valuation: Avoiding the Winner's Curse

International Business

Peter Marber
  Money Changes Everything: How Global Prosperity Is Reshaping Our Needs, Values, and Lifestyles

Fernando Robles, Françoise Simon, and Jerry Haar
  Winning Strategies for the New Latin Markets

Investments

Zvi Bodie and Michael J. Clowes
  Worry-Free Investing: A Safe Approach to Achieving Your Lifetime Goals

Harry Domash
  Fire Your Stock Analyst! Analyzing Stocks on Your Own

D. Quinn Mills
  Buy, Lie, and Sell High: How Investors Lost Out on Enron and the Internet Bubble

D. Quinn Mills
  Wheel, Deal, and Steal: Deceptive Accounting, Deceitful CEOs, and Ineffective Reforms

John Nofsinger and Kenneth Kim
  Infectious Greed: Restoring Confidence in America's Companies

John R. Nofsinger
  Investment Blunders (of the Rich and Famous)...And What You Can Learn from Them

John R. Nofsinger
  Investment Madness: How Psychology Affects Your Investing...And What to Do About It

H. David Sherman, S. David Young, and Harris Collingwood
  Profits You Can Trust: Spotting & Surviving Accounting Landmines

Leadership

Jim Despain and Jane Bodman Converse
  And Dignity for All: Unlocking Greatness through Values-Based Leadership

Marshall Goldsmith, Vijay Govindarajan, Beverly Kaye, and Albert A. Vicere
  The Many Facets of Leadership

Marshall Goldsmith, Cathy Greenberg, Alastair Robertson, and Maya Hu-Chan
  Global Leadership: The Next Generation

Management

Rob Austin and Lee Devin
Artful Making: What Managers Need to Know About How Artists Work

J. Stewart Black and Hal B. Gregersen
Leading Strategic Change: Breaking Through the Brain Barrier

William C. Byham, Audrey B. Smith, and Matthew J. Paese
Grow Your Own Leaders: How to Identify, Develop, and Retain Leadership Talent

David M. Carter and Darren Rovell
On the Ball: What You Can Learn About Business from Sports Leaders

Subir Chowdhury
Organization 21C: Someday All Organizations Will Lead this Way

Ross Dawson
Living Networks: Leading Your Company, Customers, and Partners in the Hyper-connected Economy

Charles J. Fombrun and Cees B.M. Van Riel
Fame and Fortune: How Successful Companies Build Winning Reputations

Amir Hartman
Ruthless Execution: What Business Leaders Do When Their Companies Hit the Wall

Harvey A. Hornstein
The Haves and the Have Nots: The Abuse of Power and Privilege in the Workplace… and How to Control It

Kevin Kennedy and Mary Moore
Going the Distance: Why Some Companies Dominate and Others Fail

Robin Miller
The Online Rules of Successful Companies: The Fool-Proof Guide to Building Profits

Fergus O'Connell
The Competitive Advantage of Common Sense: Using the Power You Already Have

W. Alan Randolph and Barry Z. Posner
Checkered Flag Projects: 10 Rules for Creating and Managing Projects that Win, Second Edition

Stephen P. Robbins
Decide & Conquer: Make Winning Decisions to Take Control of Your Life

Stephen P. Robbins
The Truth About Managing People…And Nothing but the Truth

Ronald Snee and Roger Hoerl
Leading Six Sigma: A Step-by-Step Guide Based on Experience with GE and Other Six Sigma Companies

Susan E. Squires, Cynthia J. Smith, Lorna McDougall, and William R. Yeack
Inside Arthur Andersen: Shifting Values, Unexpected Consequences

Jerry Weissman
Presenting to Win: The Art of Telling Your Story

Contents

CHAPTER 2   ASSESSING MARKET POTENTIAL:
ESTIMATING MARKET SIZE AND TIMING
OF ENTRY 27

Chapter 3   Strategies for Entering and Developing International Markets 61

Chapter 5 Selecting and Managing International Distributors 129

PREFACE AND ACKNOWLEDGMENTS

This book is the product of the research, teaching, and writing work associated with the International Marketing Management course on the MBA at the Harvard Business School, which I ran for six years. It is a unique benefit of working at HBS that one bridges the divide between academia and management practice, which is all too wide elsewhere in the field of marketing. I should therefore emphasize immediately the type of book this is intended to be (and the type of book it is not). This is not a textbook to aid students acquire a knowledge of the main issues in international marketing—a number of excellent such books already exist. It is rather a managerially focused book. This means the following:

- It is organized as a set of essays addressing the key challenges facing managers in international marketing, rather than as an exposition of a conceptual framework of the subject.

- Topics that are treated separately in marketing textbooks are sometimes therefore amalgamated into a single managerial issue. An example is Chapter 6, which addresses both customer management (or sales) and pricing, which in many cases are two facets of the same challenge in international business.

- The aim of the book is insight, rather than comprehensive coverage. This applies both to the topics covered—where the focus is on the key challenges facing executives—and to the conclusions reached.

Of course, I hope the book will prove of value to MBA students as well as managers, dependent upon the extent to which their studies are managerially oriented. And of course, theoretical frameworks are introduced where relevant, since all the top managers I have met are thinking managers.

The spur to writing this book is the fact that managers and students have repeatedly asked me over the years to recommend a concise, managerially focused book on international marketing. The wider context in which the book is framed consists of two principal characteristics I have observed in international companies. The first is the rapid rate at which companies are globalizing—advances in network technology and the opening up of huge new labor markets are among the drivers of this trend. The result is that companies are globalizing far faster than markets, leading to an increased risk of mismanagement in addressing those markets. The second is an older pattern—the tolerance of lower managerial standards in international operations than are demanded in home market operations. More experienced multinationals are beginning to manage their executive talent and operations on a global basis, and so address this issue, but many nevertheless, for example, overestimate the potential sales in emerging markets, and of course global management systems can produce company-driven rather than market-driven decisions.

A host of people have contributed to the ideas in this book, and I am grateful to them all. The largest group is the many hundreds of MBA students I have taught at the Harvard Business School—the interaction of bright minds tackling managerial case studies never fails to uncover new insights, and ensures that the "teacher" is also learning. Also too numerous to mention are the many company executives who have willingly lent their time and experience to my research, including the writing of many case studies. In almost all cases, these thinking managers also demonstrated a wide-ranging curiosity to learn more about a field in which others regarded them as experts. Among my colleagues at Harvard Business School, two in particular merit my gratitude for their long-running contribution to all aspects of my work. These are John Quelch, one of the pioneers of the field of international marketing and still one of its pillars, and Kash Rangan, one of the most inspirational teachers I have ever met. Both have been unstinting in their mentoring, even though it is many years since they sat on my doctoral committee. As a one-time editor myself, I must also express my thanks to Tim Moore and Russ Hall at Prentice Hall, who have been exceptional in their ability to flex on secondary administrative requirements and concentrate on the important issues of the book, to the undoubted benefit of my work.

Finally, and most importantly, I wish to thank my family. My wife Megan is always a source of all the support I need, and then more. My children Kate and Thomas, who mastered reading during the time when I was writing this, were inspirational in their excitement that I was writing a book they could read. Maybe one day…

1 MANAGE GLOBALLY, MARKET LOCALLY

This chapter has two objectives. First, it outlines the central thesis of this book—that while companies are growing larger, markets are growing smaller. The thesis puts forward the idea that what companies should pursue is global marketing management, but at a local level rather than with mass marketing programs. Second, it describes what is different about international marketing, exploring the international marketing management process and subsequently identifying key managerial guidelines for managing this tension between opposing forces.

It is a matter of common observation both that the world's largest companies are growing in size, as measured by sales revenues rather than their increasingly volatile stock market valuations, and that most of these companies rely on international markets for an increasing proportion of those revenues. It can therefore be said that companies are globalizing. This results in their products being distributed in more and more countries, and this in turn provokes many commentators to conclude that markets are globalizing.

In fact, the most striking development in most markets is that, far from consolidating, they are fragmenting, as information technology allows companies to move ever closer towards "segment of one," addressing customers individually rather

in response to globaliz. c~~ountr~~ companies are fragmenting.

than in aggregate segments or markets. It is likely that, in the more developed economies at least, the era of mass marketing has passed its peak, and that direct or "one-to-one" or "relationship" marketing is becoming a reality for more companies and consumers. The fact that a well-traveled consumer can find the same hamburger or brand of shampoo in many different countries does not constitute market globalization—it merely points to increased international distribution of those brands. True, globalization involves the same competitive structure across different countries and, therefore, the consolidation of industries worldwide. The opposite is in fact happening, as research shows: while companies are globalizing, the concentration of most industries is decreasing. Put in simple language, the internationalization of the world's largest corporations has stimulated competition, not stifled it, and consumers end up with greater choice after multinational companies (MNCs) enter their markets. The MNCs grow in sales, but not in global market share.

So, what are the distinctive characteristics of international marketing as opposed to domestic or single-market marketing? To date, the marketing field has not recognized international marketing as a distinct theoretical subdomain, but as a context characterized principally by differences of degree, rather than kind, in areas such as consumer behavior and the regulation of business—comparable, say, to financial services marketing or sports marketing. By contrast, executives in international companies intuitively know that international marketing is a different challenge, and they accordingly place a high value on international experience, frequently making it a prerequisite for senior level appointment.

This is important because most companies struggle to make as much profit in international markets as in their home markets, the so-called "foreign investment profitability gap." This gap is counter-intuitive, since entry into international markets is often regarded by expanding companies as "gravy" in the sense that it is incremental business, leveraging existing assets such as products and brand names, and it is undertaken without intensive capital exposure through indirect means such as local

*frequent underestimate of
amt. of work req. on
entry*

independent agents or distributors. It is this "marginalizing" mindset that might be the reason for the frequent underperformance of companies in international markets—companies sometimes tolerate managerial standards in the international operations that are, frankly, lower than those expected in their domestic operations. The low performance, for example, is tolerated rather than made the subject of intensive turn-around efforts, as would be the case at home. Similarly, many companies struggling through the crises of the international distributor life cycle (see Chapter 5) exercise complex and sophisticated distributor control systems in their domestic market that are never applied in international operations.

Despite these challenges, the benefits of globalization for a firm can be significant in two broad areas. First, size matters. Larger companies with operations on a global scale can gain an advantage in production economies of scale, buying power in everything from raw materials through to advertising campaigns, and in the ability to attract the brightest and most ambitious managerial talent. In situations in which no single company enjoys sustainable product superiority (an increasingly common situation in contemporary markets), the advantages of size become even more telling. The second benefit of globalization is that greater international reach increases exponentially the range of situations, ideas, and competition to which the company is exposed, thus endowing it with a far greater ability to learn, innovate, and develop. Here too, contemporary markets, often mature and intensely competitive, are making this an increasingly important source of advantage and are rewarding "learning organizations."

The challenge of international marketing, then, is to capture the benefits of globalization without sacrificing the local market responsiveness required as the era of mass marketing wanes. What is required, in other words, is global marketing management, but not global marketing. The aim of the managerial process that is global marketing must be to deliver marketing solutions that lack nothing in terms of local relevance and immediacy—given the fragmenting character of most markets. This is something like the long-established adage

*global marketing mngmt is req. due
to fragmentation of the market.*

"think globally, act locally," a piece of wisdom with which everybody agrees but which almost nobody claims to have mastered. This book attempts to help you progress towards that state by enhancing understanding of the challenges of international marketing, providing guidelines for improving the quality of management in international operations, and outlining those areas in which global management must aim to produce local actions and benefits.

THE INTERNATIONAL MARKETING GENIE ESCAPES FROM THE BOTTLE

At the turn of the twenty-first century, the spotlight of public attention has suddenly and unexpectedly turned on international marketing as an issue of great social, cultural, and political consequence. Of course, for the previous couple of decades at least, it has been recognized as a vital issue for business leaders. CEOs in the developed world have increasingly stressed the importance of international expansion to their companies' growth as they approached saturation in their domestic markets. As more country-markets became available through trade liberalization, and companies could manage their operations from afar through advances in communications and operations, most large corporations chased these opportunities with a fervor that occasionally resulted in something like a gold rush atmosphere. What has changed is that international marketing has now been regarded from the perspective of the consumer, not the business. The boot is on the other foot. And now international marketing is widely portrayed as a force for evil in the world. It is therefore wise to address these arguments at the outset.

One of the strongest claims of the emergent antiglobalization movement is that consumers do not want to be offered the same products and services everywhere in the world (or to be marketed to in the same way) and that the efforts of multinational companies to do so threaten the cultural diversity of the world—and therefore damage social welfare. Not only is

now regarded from perspective of consumer

this bland homogeneity objected to, but also it is argued that it happens to have latched onto the worst aspects of modern business: western or American marketing, with its image-driven brands, mass-produced goods, and creeping commercialization and sponsorship of everything. This demonized version of international marketing was labeled "McWorld" by the political scientist Benjamin Barber:[1]

> McWorld is a product of popular culture driven by expansionist commerce. Its template is American, its form style. Its goods are as much about images as matériel, an aesthetic as well as a product line.... There is no activity more intrinsically globalizing than trade, no ideology less interested in nations than capitalism, no challenge to frontiers more audacious than the market.... [Multinational companies'] customers are not citizens of a particular nation or members of a parochial clan: they belong to the universal tribe of consumers defined by needs and wants that are ubiquitous, if not by nature then by the cunning of advertising. A consumer is a consumer is a consumer.... Modern transnational corporations in quest of global markets cannot really comprehend "foreign policy" because the word foreign has no meaning to the ambitious global businessperson ... they do not find foreign countries foreign: as far as production and consumption are concerned, there is only one world and it is McWorld.

The two ways in which Barber suggests that international marketing damages society (by undermining the power of democratic nation states and by replacing national cultures with the anonymous consumerism of McWorld) will be unrecognizable to any executive working inside a multinational corporation. To begin with, the power of national governments over corporations remains absolute: they can regulate, tax, help, or hinder companies in any way they see fit in any country of the world. Indeed, the regulatory posture of national governments towards foreign companies is one of the principal criteria used by companies when assessing the attractiveness of markets

---

1. Benjamin Barber, *Jihad vs. McWorld: How Globalism and Tribalism Are Reshaping the World* (New York: Random House, 1995).

before entry. Moreover, all transactions (the building blocks of markets) remain nationally bounded: all orders have to be booked at a local level according to the laws of one country; all payments have to be invoiced, paid, and accounted for, including taxation considerations, at a local level; and even the people making the transaction have to be employed, paid, and taxed according to national regulations. From this perspective, international business is in fact no more than the aggregation of a large number of local transactions.

As regards the undermining of local tastes with imported artificial desires, once again most international marketing executives would not recognize this problem. It is the divergence of tastes that is more striking, not their homogeneity. This persists even in product categories that are usually regarded as not at all culture bound. In the 1990s, for example, all manufacturers of laundry detergents attempted to switch consumers in southern Europe from bulky powders to the newer compact forms, such as gels, liquids, and capsules, which had been so successful in the north. This was not a manipulation of tastes, but a rational appeal: the greater concentration of these product forms produced the environmental benefits of reduced quantities of raw materials and packaging, which had been well received in northern European markets. Moreover, retailers as well as manufacturers were behind the move because the new product forms required less storage and shelf space, thus reducing costs in the distribution system. And yet, despite this, southern European consumers remained attached to their "fluffies" (as bulk powders are known in the trade), and the industry eventually gave up in its attempts to introduce compacts in those markets. As one industry executive commented, "It was one of our biggest mistakes. Consumers in southern Europe were not interested. They like their big boxes!" [2]

It is probably true that there was something of a love affair with western brands in the early 1990s, as many of the major

---

2.   David J. Arnold, "Henkel Detergents Division," Harvard Business School case study 9-502-019. Boston: Harvard Business School Publishing.

emerging economies such as China, India, and Russia were opened to western multinationals. In hindsight, this was largely a burst of novelty buying and a manifestation of pent-up demand resulting from decades of unavailability. Not only are consumers in those markets now starting to display a liking and respect for many local brands, but there are also emerging strong local competitors who launch and develop new local brands that challenge the previous ascendancy of multinational brands as the best value propositions on offer in the market.

Were it true, the argument that international marketing damages society by reducing variety would not be without merit. As will be argued in this book, there is indeed precious little evidence that consumers demand global brands (except perhaps in a few product categories), and so it seems likely that international businesses are the main beneficiaries of any globalization. In fact, the evidence available supports the opposite view (the argument that would be espoused by most economists and business executives), which is that free international trade does improve the economic condition of all involved in the long run and that international marketing increases variety and choice rather than decreasing it.

Of course, at a market level, it is also true that in the long run, the beneficiaries of open markets are the end consumers rather than the corporations supplying them. Indeed, this is the principal justification of competitive open markets, as opposed to command economies or other regulated forms of value creation and exchange. This is amply demonstrated by the "dot-com" boom and bust, in which many Internet-based companies created huge value for end consumers, whose lives have been significantly enhanced by the Internet. But, these companies have struggled enormously to capture any of the value for themselves. The number of markets in which competition has intensified and technological innovation has slowed has been increasing in recent decades in developed economies, and this maturation of many markets results in ever improving value propositions for end consumers, who get more for their money in categories ranging from checking accounts to cars. From this perspective, the spurt of apparent globalization as consolidation in emerging economies is merely a short-term phenomenon on the longer road to a more open, fragmented, and consumer-oriented market, characterized by greater choice.

THE EVIDENCE ON GLOBALIZATION OF MARKETS

In examining the evidence, globalization is not merely international availability of the same products, but it is also greater concentration or hegemony on the part of those products. This development would indeed constitute a threat to cultural diversity and smaller local vendors, as identified by the anti-globalization movement. So, has globalization resulted in higher levels of industry concentration and thus reduced choice for consumers? Empirical research suggests that the opposite is true. Economists Pankaj Ghemawat and Fariborz Ghadar measured concentration levels for the last few decades by compiling industry-level Herfindahl Index figures, a measure of industry concentration, and concluded that "in the overwhelming majority of industries looked at, global concentration had fallen in the postwar period."[3] Concentration levels peaked in many cases immediately after World War II, when U.S. firms were dominant, and many other economies lay in ruins. Since then, innovation and economic growth has resulted in decreased levels of concentration, with governments sometimes actively protecting local companies. According to Ghemawat, the evidence indicates that globalization has proliferated rather than pruned the number of varieties available to consumers.[4]

The recent research of another leading economist in the field, Alan Rugman, has been published under the telling title

---

3. "Testing the Logic of Cross-Border Mergers," *Financial Times*, June 8, 2000, and "The Dubious Logic of Global Mega-Mergers," *Harvard Business Review*, July–August 2000.

4. Pankaj Ghemawat, "Global vs. Local Products: A Case Study and a Model." Harvard Business School Working Paper Series, No. 02-059, 2002. Boston, MA: Harvard Business School.

of *The End of Globalization*.[5] He demonstrates that trade flows between the major "Triad" markets of NAFTA, the European Union, and Japan are dwarfed by the trade flows within each regional bloc. He concludes, "Far from taking place in a single global market, most business activity by large firms takes place in regional blocks. There is no uniform spread of American market capitalism nor are global markets becoming homogenized." The implication for international marketing is that for "most manufacturing ... and all services, strategies of national responsiveness are required."

This scholarly, empirical research is supported by observation of trends in the business press. Many companies are seeking to localize their operations. Perhaps the most significant is the volte-face conducted by Coca-Cola's new Chairman and CEO Douglas Daft, after his appointment in 2000. Coca-Cola is regularly ranked as the world's most valuable brand,[6] making it not only a consumer icon but a bellwether for global companies. Daft's own account of what global marketing means is worth pondering. He argues that while "consolidation and centralized control" were probably appropriate during the company's expansion of the 1970s and 1980s, things have changed:[7]

> So, as the century was drawing to a close, the world had changed course, and we had not. The world was demanding greater flexibility, responsiveness and local sensitivity, while we were further centralizing decision-making and standardizing our practices, moving further away from our traditional multi-local approach.... And what we learned was something simple, yet powerful: that the next big evolutionary step of "going global" now has to be "going local".... Accomplishing that in the 21st century will require great creativity.... We will not abandon the benefits of being global.

In summary, the evidence available does not support the idea that markets are globalizing.

---

5. Alan M. Rugman, *The End of Globalization* (London: Random House, 2000).
6. "The Best Global Brands," *BusinessWeek*, August 6, 2001.
7. Douglas Daft, "Back to Classic Coke," *Financial Times*, March 27, 2000.

THE (RISE AND) FALL
OF MASS MARKETING

In fact, markets are fragmenting, not consolidating. An influential paper by Robert Blattberg and John Deighton in 1991 gave wide currency and validity to the ideas of "interactive marketing" and "the age of addressability," and predicted that the core marketing asset would become a customer database driven by "an electronic marketer with as much flexibility as the average human salesperson, a better memory, and a talent for the most mind-numbingly repetitive tasks."[8] Just as they predicted, we have witnessed since then (in the more technologically advanced economies at least) an unbroken increase in the extent to which companies can customize their communications, and sometimes their products and services, to "markets of one."

The comparison with the human salesperson is significant because it highlights the fact that markets are merely concepts, and artificial ones at that, while the interaction between a seller and a buyer is real and is the natural state of affairs. If we understand markets as aggregations of demand, it becomes clear that they are a compromise. A company directs its efforts at the average of its target market or segment, but it can only expect to hit its target if all the customers need and want the same thing—an unlikely situation. The following are two respects in which "markets" and "marketing" are compromises:

ECONOMIC

In an ideal world, companies would use individual salespeople for all their selling because this is the most powerful method of influencing a potential customer. In practice, companies only utilize personal selling when the likely order is large enough to cover the high cost of this selling method. In other situations, companies resort to less expensive but less directly persuasive

---

8.   Robert Blattberg and John Deighton, "Interactive Marketing: Exploiting the Age of Addressability," *Sloan Management Review*, Fall 1991.

selling methods such as direct mail and advertising. This economic compromise also applies to production (i.e., the mass production of identical products for a range of customers) and communications (mass media such as advertising rather than direct customized communications).

INFORMATION

The core principle of marketing is that a company is a reactive agent, stimulated by information on the needs and wants of a customer. In practice, market research is mostly an exercise in minimizing variations in demand from a sample group to an average that forms an acceptable target for mass marketing. This is not only because of the expense of gathering information on an individual basis, but it is also because of the inability of many customers to remember or articulate their preferences. With advanced information technology, the purchase and consumption pattern of individual consumers can be recorded as the basis for a truly interactive marketing process—online and catalog retailers and many business-to-business marketers demonstrate the power of this model.

The key point here is that the fragmentation of markets into segments of one is not a phase in the evolution of the profession, but it is rather the natural state of affairs that can be expected to prevail in the future. Indeed, the rise of mass marketing is a relatively recent phenomenon, occurring mostly in the twentieth century in a period that saw increasing returns to scale in manufacturing, communications, and distribution—returns that were passed on to customers in the form of ever improving value propositions. Advancing technology is making it increasingly possible to achieve simultaneously the benefits of scale and one-to-one marketing.

It is ironic that at a time when most companies are investing effort in taking their marketing closer to individual customers, international companies are being criticized for driving the world towards a bland homogeneity in which individual recognition and taste are obliterated. Any company that enters international markets with this strategy in mind is swimming against the tide of marketing and is likely to fail.

THE MANAGERIAL CHALLENGE— MOST COMPANIES UNDERPERFORM IN INTERNATIONAL MARKETS

The Templeton Global Performance Index, an ongoing research study that examines the relative profitability of domestic and international operations in the world's largest multinational firms, highlights what it labels the "foreign investment profitability gap." This gap, between the profitability of domestic and international sales, reached its highest level to date in 1999, when foreign operations represented 43 percent of sales but only 33 percent of profit across the sample companies, prompting the researchers to conclude that "many of the world's biggest multinational companies have suffered continuing declines in profitability—and, in some cases, losses—on their foreign operations.... [T]he findings show that many large multinational corporations are not particularly good at managing their foreign activities, and that strong core competencies do not guarantee international commercial success."[9] As the data in Figure 1–1 demonstrates, this gap has been evident for most of the period from 1989–2000, although it varies considerably. Although this gap had been closed by 2000, it should be noted that this was "largely the result of exceptional performance in foreign markets by a handful of firms," and that 70 percent of the sample was still below the median in terms of profit performance in foreign markets. It is also clear from this data that a number of firms had reacted to earlier performance problems not by turning around their international operations but by closing down the least profitable national units and putting the brakes on international expansion. As the recessionary pressure built through 2002, even the most committed of global marketers, such as McDonald's, took the decision to retreat from some international markets,

---

9. Michael V. Gestrin, Rory F. Knight, and Alan M. Rugman, *Templeton Global Performance Index 2001* (Oxford: Templeton College, Oxford University).

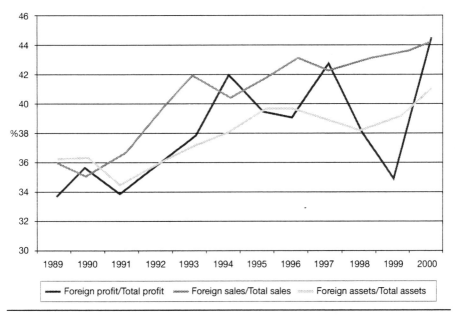

| | Foreign profit/Total profit | Foreign sales/Total sales | Foreign assets/Total assets |

FIGURE 1–1 The Foreign Investment Profitability Gap *(Source: Templeton Global Performance Index)*

announcing in November 2002 the closing down of stores around the world and exiting several countries entirely.

There are a number of mistakes that are repeatedly made by even experienced companies in international markets, which in many cases will explain the poor profit performance:

OVERESTIMATION OF MARKET POTENTIAL

Throughout the 1990s, the same unrealistic optimism regarding market size was evident both in international business and in "new economy" ventures and the "dot-com" bubble. Difficult though it is to estimate the size of some international markets, especially in less developed economies, due to paucity of information, there is little excuse for the almost casual way in which some major corporations decided to commit substantial capital on the basis of no more than a vision of the future importance of a country. This subject is dealt with in detail in the next chapter.

FAILURE TO COMMIT TO THE MARKET

It is common for internationalizing companies to adopt a low-risk approach to international market entry, employing local agents or distributors to bear the financial risk of local operations and managing the venture from outside the market, with occasional inspection visits by a regional or corporate executive. There are rational reasons for this: the low level of initial sales will not cover the fixed cost of a national operating unit, and the risk of operating in an uncertain country environment justifies caution. However, there will always come a point at which further growth cannot be achieved without further investment, and companies routinely wait too long before making such an investment. In many cases, this investment is needed to develop local products that will take the company beyond the market skimming position that results from merely distributing the existing range of products from other markets. Too often, one sees companies stuck in this skimming position long after entry.

manage from outside the market.

MISMANAGEMENT OF LOCAL PARTNERS

The series of crises described in Chapter 5 as the international distributor life cycle is a source of repeated discomfort and business disruption to almost all international marketing companies. Executives in those companies will often blame the shortcomings of the "typical distributor," and yet the multinational is usually equally to blame for the mismatch in expectations and capabilities. The most common mistake is overdelegation of authority to a local partner who, despite being a distributor, is being asked to act as the *de facto* marketing department of the company for that country.

overdelegation of power to local partners

FAILURE TO READ MARKET DEVELOPMENT PATTERNS

Business growth in an international market should be more rapid that the original growth in the company's home market, given the accumulated experience and assets that the company can bring to bear. Despite this, it is common to see companies slow in reacting to growth and failing to appreciate the need for additional product lines, or new products altogether, or entry into new segments or regions within the country. It is ironic that while most companies suffer from product proliferation in their home markets, they frequently carry too few products in international markets. In too many cases, multinationals adopt a reactive approach to international market development rather than having a plan for market expansion based upon previous experience in other markets.

These mistakes are examined in detail in later chapters of this book. First, however, it is important to place these issues in a more general framework for the challenge of managing international marketing. That process begins by identifying what differences the international situation makes to marketing management.

WHAT IS DIFFERENT ABOUT INTERNATIONAL MARKETING?

Consistent with the earlier argument that markets are growing smaller while businesses are growing larger, most of the challenges of international marketing are organizational. The output of these managerial processes, the marketing offer to the target customers, must remain focused and compelling in international markets as in the domestic market. But those managerial processes must also take into account the distinctive dynamics of international markets.

THE WIDE RANGE OF MARKETING FUNCTIONS DEMANDED OF THE LOCAL OPERATING UNIT OR DISTRIBUTOR

A national distributor for an international corporation is generally responsible not just for the conventional distribution functions, but also for marketing strategy functions for the country-market. The "distributor" is the *de facto* branch or marketing company of the multinational in that country for two reasons. First, the distributor will usually have been granted an exclusive agency for the market—even though this is never done in the domestic market. This expanded responsibility is granted in order to encourage investment in market development, and it also provides easier accountability from the international company's perspective. Second, international companies are generally concerned to minimize their risk during the market entry phase, and so they commit fewer resources to building their business than would be the case at home, delegating the risk instead to their local partner. Although these two factors call for a local partner with the marketing capability to build a market from scratch, multinationals in fact frequently select partners more akin to traditional distributors in terms of skill set and business philosophy, and it is their lack of strategic marketing capability that often results in a plateau in performance a few years after market entry.

RAPID GROWTH OF BUSINESS

International markets are characterized by a faster and more conscious evolution through the growth curve of business development than in the "first-time-around" domestic market. The evolution, from low-commitment market entry through local business development to consolidation into a global network, accelerates with international experience from a more laissez-faire attitude in early years of international operation to a deliberate and more forceful approach as the firm attaches greater importance to its international business. This requires a planned approach to sequential product line introductions, investment in additional sales force and promotional campaigns, and managerial recruitment.

MULTIMARKET DECISIONS

Once a firm is operating in several country-markets, it inevitably starts comparing them in terms of performance and transferring policies, products, and people among them. The result is that decisions are made on the basis of system optimization rather than market optimization—or simply in the belief that what was learned in one market is transferable to another. This can result in the inappropriate transfer of mental models from one market to another (e.g., "It's always best to stick with distributors for the first few years") as well as the transfer of effective learning (e.g., "Look for signs of unfulfilled demand at lower price points"). This can also result in different strategic objectives being set by different players in the same market.

The key to understanding the distinctive challenges of international distribution is to take an evolutionary perspective. As the business grows in an international market, marketing strategy evolves through a series of phases, each requiring additional management resources, new skills, and financial investment. The fit among product line, positioning, and distributor might be perfect at the point of market entry, but it might quickly disappear and require a revised marketing strategy after only a short period in the market.

focus on evolutionary view of market.

THE DYNAMICS OF INTERNATIONAL COMPETITION

The ability to read international marketing situations depends upon an identification of the drivers of an individual company's strategy. There is likely to be much greater divergence among the players in international competition than in a single-market situation simply because the underlying objective for market participation can differ so greatly. Figure 1–2 provides a framework for analyzing these dynamics.

The drivers of internationalization can be categorized into market, industry, and company factors.

MARKET

Consumers. There are two ways in which consumers might value international marketing (i.e., might derive benefit from the fact that what they are buying is marketed in a similar way in other countries). First, to the extent that consumers

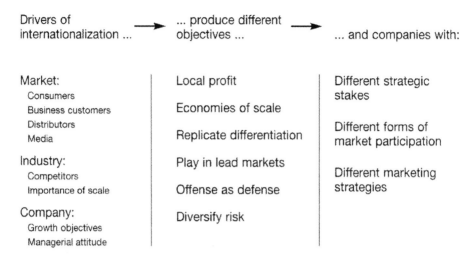

Drivers of internationalization ...	... produce different objectives ...	... and companies with:
Market: Consumers Business customers Distributors Media	Local profit Economies of scale Replicate differentiation	Different strategic stakes Different forms of market participation
Industry: Competitors Importance of scale	Play in lead markets Offense as defense	Different marketing strategies
Company: Growth objectives Managerial attitude	Diversify risk	

FIGURE 1–2   Dynamics of International Competition

are mobile, it can be assumed that they value consistency in what they buy as they travel. Thus, consumers who are traveling away from their home country are more likely to purchase a familiar brand or package and are more likely to respond to a familiar advertisement than to experiment with an unknown local brand. While this seems logical, the extent to which consumers purchase staple items while traveling is almost certainly overstated by advocates of this frequently cited "world citizen" argument. While the world travel market has certainly expanded hugely, most trips remain a week or less in duration, and accordingly, most purchases are of gifts, the one category in which unknown local items might be attractive. With regard to longer foreign travels, it is worth noting that the mobility of the world's population has not yet reached the high point of 1900, when 3.1 percent of the world's population was living outside their country of birth, compared with 2.4 percent in 2000.

The second way in which consumers might value international consistency in marketing is when globalism constitutes part of the brand's appeal. In a restricted number of product categories, such as luxury goods, a brand's appeal can undoubtedly be enhanced by associations with cosmopolitanism, adoption by the "international jet set," and the influence of global brand leadership. These attributes, mostly image based, are also evident in some youth-based products, such as video games or pop music merchandising. This dynamic underpins the fact that the premium and youth segments are among the most globally homogenized of consumer categories.

Business Customers. When a firm is marketing to another business, as opposed to end consumers, it is very likely indeed that its market has internationalized. Companies are far more international than consumers. In many cases, this internationalization is driven primarily by functions other than marketing, such as the relocation of manufacturing or the globalization of procurement in order to achieve economies of scale in purchasing. At the same time, recent years have seen a shift in procurement policies in many companies towards strategic partnerships with a reduced number of suppliers, which produces account concentration on the vendor side. These two factors combined mean that in many business-to-business markets, international marketing is a prerequisite for participation in the market because many customers will not consider a supplier unless it can offer sales and service support in all the countries in which it operates.

This follows logically from the central premise of this book—that companies have become considerably more global in their scope, although end consumers have not.

Distribution Channels and Communication Media. Distributors have been among the last business sector to internationalize, given their capital intensity and their embeddedness in complex local supply systems. Recently, however, there have been substantial investments in building global networks by retailers such as Carrefour, Royal Ahold and Wal-Mart; retail chains such as Benetton or The Gap; logistics providers such as Federal Express or DHL; and financial intermediaries such as Citigroup and HSBC. Similarly, there has been significant internationalization in communication media, so that channels such as CNN or MTV are known in almost all countries of the world. These developments are in effect an internationalization of the infrastructure of marketing, and they facilitate levels of international coordination that were previously impossible. A manufacturer such as

Procter & Gamble (P&G) can now enter international agreements with its largest customer, Wal-Mart: Procter & Gamble achieves international distribution via a single agreement; Wal-Mart simplifies its buying process by consolidating previously separate orders, achieving larger volumes, and pressing for greater consistency in the products it stocks in different countries. A brand manufacturer like Procter & Gamble can now also run international promotions or advertising campaigns or sponsor international events.

INDUSTRY

One of the strongest drivers of internationalization of marketing is competitive pressure—the fact that a firm may have competitors that operate internationally. A marketing purist might argue that this is irrelevant—that a consumer will make a choice from the alternative products offered without considering whether it is offered in other countries. While this argument is valid in its own limited terms, it misses the critical point—the nature of the offer made to the consumer will itself have been influenced by the degree of internationalization of the manufacturer. If the same product is offered in several countries, for example, one might expect economies of scale to have led to lower production cost than a local product. This can either be passed through to the consumer in the form of a lower price or retained by the manufacturer to allocate to trade promotions (giving it better distribution) or consumer promotions (enhancing its market power through higher awareness, for example). A company with international operations can achieve inter-market benefits by, for example, subsidizing one market with profits from another, shifting production from country to country to take advantage of lower costs, buying raw materials from the lowest cost source as prices fluctuate in world markets, or dealing with best-in-class suppliers even though they are located in different countries. Any of these benefits of the "global chess game"[10] can be translated into advantages in the marketing mix deployed in any single country.

---

10. Thomas Hout, Michael Porter, and Eileen Rudden, "How Global Companies Win Out," *Harvard Business Review*, November–December 1982.

COMPANY

Although it is a less tangible factor, one should never underestimate the importance of the attitude adopted by senior executives towards the international operations of their company. Some of the largest global corporations owe their status to early internationalization undertaken by leaders with the drive to expand into other countries when their competitors never even considered such a move. King Gillette, founder of Gillette, was just such a leader. He wrote a book entitled *The Global Corporation* in the early years of the twentieth century, when such ideas were radical, and led his company into markets that many of his competitors had barely heard of. Any consultant or experienced executive who is acquainted with several international companies will know first hand that culture and attitude towards international operations, towards the level of risk tolerated in new investments, and even towards individual countries can explain much of a company's internationalization pattern.

The following drivers can produce quite distinct objectives in the market and therefore quite different strategic stakes:

LOCAL PROFIT MAXIMIZATION

This default option can be expected to produce competitive behavior no different from that of a purely local player. Typically, this strategy is not adopted until the international firm has been in the market for a considerable period, and has had its own subsidiary established.

ECONOMIES OF SCALE

Since one major benefit of internationalization is increased sales volumes, there exists significant potential for achieving greater economies of scale if the extra sales volumes (i.e., the international sales) are of the same product type. This could then be translated into a resource advantage over a local player with lower sales levels. This objective will clearly push a company towards a policy of global product standardization, of course, and it therefore depends upon market acceptance of this universal product. The local player is likely to build a strategy around local product and "local player" positioning.

LEVERAGE DIFFERENTIATION

If a company has what it regards as a superior value proposition because of product advantage or a superior service operation, it can be expected to regard international markets as incremental sales opportunities and, as a result, to pursue rapid expansion through low commitment methods of participation. Fast food chains, for example, pursue this "replication strategy" in the belief that their unique and differentiated offer has wide appeal: the franchise form of participation employed by many such companies offers the fastest expansion with relatively low financial risk and works because the companies pursue little adaptation of their core offer. This is, in effect, an "export strategy" in that it alters little of the marketing mix and merely extends the arena in which the firm competes.

PLAY IN LEAD MARKETS

In many product categories, certain countries are regarded as lead markets, with the most advanced products on offer, the most sophisticated customers, and the world's leading provider companies all present. It is in such markets that innovations in the product will be developed and first brought to market. For example, the United States is regarded as the lead market for entertainment, Japan for wireless Internet devices, and France and Italy for luxury and fashion products. A global company will usually want to participate in the lead market with the objectives of developing its capabilities through the innovation that takes place in the market and the competitive goal of participating at the leading edge of the market. Such objectives might take precedence over local profit maximization, and so the local unit of the company might have different performance targets and a different role within the global network—with added global responsibility as the source of new product ideas.

OFFENSE AS DEFENSE

It is common for an international company to enter the home market of a major competitor as a direct competitive move (i.e., not because of a judgment on the attractiveness of that market). The firm's objective will be to cause maximum disruption to its competitor's domestic market operations and so to tie up significant resources there that might otherwise have been deployed in the international arena. In such circumstances, one might expect to see aggressive marketing policies in areas such as price and sales promotions—policies that are intended to maximize market share rather than local profit.

THE DYNAMICS OF INTERNATIONAL COMPETITION—AN EXAMPLE

An example of several international dynamics at work is the case of Arcelik, the white goods (appliances such as refrigerators and washing machines) subsidiary of the Turkish conglomerate Koc Holdings.[11] As part of a huge and dominant local conglomerate that is well established in Turkey, Arcelik had enjoyed a 50–70 percent market share in all categories of white goods in Turkey. With its domestic market established and with little room left for growth, Arcelik began looking to overseas markets as a source of growth. At the same time, western companies expanding internationally frequently placed Turkey as a high priority market, given its size and its strategic position between East and West. Just as Arcelik began exporting to neighboring countries in the Middle East, North Africa, and Central Asia, it faced a new competitive threat as Bosch Siemens, a German global leader in this category, acquired one of its smaller Turkish rivals as a means of market entry. The way that this competition played out over the following years illustrates several of these different objectives:

- Arcelik decided to enter Germany, the home market of Bosch Siemens, for two reasons. First, it was a competitive attack on its new rival on its home turf ("offense as defense"). Second, Germany is generally regarded as the

---

11. Robin Root and John A. Quelch, "Koc Holdings: Arcelik White Goods," Harvard Business School case study 9-598-033. Boston, MA: Harvard Business School Publishing.

world's lead market for white goods, and Arcelik therefore aimed to develop further the capabilities it would require as it entered new markets and competed with the world's leaders in the field.

- The German operation of Arcelik was therefore given two distinctive roles. First, in order to provide meaningful competition to Bosch in its home market, Arcelik had to adopt aggressive penetration marketing policies that were oriented around price competition and frequent promotions. Second, as the company's "eyes and ears" in the world's lead market, it had to establish mechanisms to transfer learning from Germany back to the wider corporation.

- It would have been quite inappropriate for Arcelik to participate in Germany indirectly (e.g., through a distributor or local licensee). Given that a major objective of entering Germany was to learn from the world's most advanced competitors and consumers, an indirect participation strategy would have created more distance between the company and the market—thus reducing learning. With the objective of learning, then, Arcelik was likely to commit resources to establishing its own subsidiary in Germany at the time of market entry, as opposed to the usual market entry strategy of entering the market via a local independent agent or distributor to minimize financial exposure at a time when sales were low.

- By contrast, Arcelik's entry into the central Asian republics, such as Kazakhstan and Uzbekistan, was undertaken with the objective of business growth and profit. These were emerging markets, with relatively low levels of demand but high potential and little competition; in addition, long-standing cultural links between the central Asian republics and Turkey made the managerial and marketing challenge less for Arcelik than many of its global competitors. In such a case, one would expect Arcelik to perhaps enter the market in the conventional indirect manner but eventually to switch to its own subsidiary and perhaps develop a new line of entry-level products to help stimulate growth in these low-income economies.

SUMMARY

The art of international marketing management is understanding how to reap the benefits of a global network—size and learning—without jeopardizing responsiveness to local marketing conditions. After a period of mass-marketing, we are entering an era when the basic principle of marketing, that a company should start by understanding the needs and wants of its customers as closely as possible, is once again in the ascendancy. Ironically, this occurs at a period when substantial public attention is directed towards the globalization of markets, meaning the convergence of consumer preference around the world, and towards a consolidation of providers into a small clique of multinationals offering western mass-market brands. In fact, the globalization of markets is a myth, and convergence, which never progressed far, has passed its peak, as consumers reassert their local heritage through purchasing patterns. The only arena in which markets can be said to have globalized is in the business-to-business context. This produces its own distinctive challenges, especially with regard to price maintenance, and it should be noted that here, too, the dominant pattern is not consolidation but fragmentation—into dedicated customer-centric units that operate internationally.

The best international marketing managers know where to draw the line between global and local decisions. In addition, the best international marketing companies insist on the highest managerial standards in areas such as market assessment and the management of local distributors, challenges unique to the international marketing context. The remainder of this book addresses the specific challenges of international marketing from the perspective of the international company.

2 ASSESSING MARKET POTENTIAL: ESTIMATING MARKET SIZE AND TIMING OF ENTRY

Although the Internet boom grabbed all the headlines for speculative excess and managerial misjudgment in the 1990s, there was another decision-making arena in which western executives seriously underperformed—market assessment and entry decisions, particularly with regard to large emerging markets such as China. In a retrospective commentary on what it describes as an "infatuation" *The Economist* commented, "Few companies are stupid, but many have behaved stupidly in China."[1] Similarly, Harvard economist Pankaj Ghemawat reflects that "companies routinely exaggerate the attractiveness of foreign markets."[2] Not only have many foreign market investments proven unprofitable, but many multinationals are now trimming back their foreign investments. For many, this is an unprecedented retrenchment in the previously uninterrupted internationalization of their business.

How can such sophisticated companies make such a fundamental error as misreading the size of a large market? It must be acknowledged, of course, that the first phase of the

---

1. "Infatuation's End," *The Economist*, September 25, 1999.
2. Pankaj Ghemawat, "Distance Still Matters: The Hard Reality of Global Expansion," *Harvard Business Review* (September 2001): 3–11.

process of internationalization—the decision to enter a foreign market—is perhaps the most challenging of all. To assess the potential and dynamics of a market from outside (often in the absence of reliable market research) is obviously a difficult case of decision making under uncertainty. That companies so frequently make occasional mistakes is therefore perhaps not surprising. Look a little deeper into the decision-making process, however, and one often finds that the decision was taken in such a haphazard fashion that the company gave itself little chance of having made the right call about which market to enter. Instead, many companies succumbed to an expansionary zeal in which attention to rigorous market analysis was less prominent in decision making than visions of huge potential sales growth in new markets and a belief that there was a limited window of opportunity for entering the new markets and staking a claim on future riches.

Thus, for example, western car makers overinvested in China, lured by the country's population and no doubt partly motivated by the threat of saturation in their established western markets. While some were acting in the belief that they could preempt competition and gain first-mover advantage, "through the 1980s and 1990s, China disappointed. Carmakers came, made losses, argued with their Chinese partners, lamented the leakage of their technologies, and often left again."[3] Despite this, new foreign investment in 2003 was estimated by the *China Economic Review* to be creating at least 20 percent overcapacity relative to growth in consumer demand.[4] Similarly, Nestlé and Unilever, two of the world's giants in the food business, invested heavily in the ice cream market in Saudi Arabia, judging the market to be highly attractive by using established measures such as the proportion of youth in the population and the climate of the country. Yet, by 2001, both firms had exited the market, unable to reach profitability in the face of cultural barriers such as the inability of women to drive to supermarkets and low acceptance of ice

3.   "The Great Leap Forward," *The Economist*, January 30, 2003.
4.   Ibid.

cream as an eat-at-home dessert.[5] Note that in both these examples, the companies involved were experienced international firms with a cadre of seasoned international executives. Both focused on top-line indicators, such as population, as a guide to market potential and underestimated the difficulties of market-specific factors such as regulatory or cultural barriers to growth, or underdeveloped distribution channels.

This chapter examines the two critical decisions involved at this stage of internationalization. The first is the choice of which market to enter—particularly the forecasting of market potential; the second is the timing of entry—particularly the question of first-mover advantage, one of the most prevalent items of conventional wisdom in the managerial and investment communities.

need to focus on market specific factors.

PITFALLS IN FOREIGN MARKET ASSESSMENT

There are a number of traps into which companies can fall when assessing foreign market entry. The first is to exaggerate the size and attractiveness of a market. In the internationalization boom of the 1990s, "strategic visions" were used to justify investments based upon flimsy analysis of markets, such as those based upon national populations (hence, China could be viewed as the world's most attractive market). From the late 1980s onwards, a number of large markets were opened up, either as communist states collapsed or as governments began the process of economic liberalization. From 1985–1998, at least 54 countries became "open" and joined the global economy, increasing the share of the world's population in "open" economies from 22 percent to 76 percent, an increase of over 3 billion people.[6] Faced by maturing markets in the developed world, western

5. David J. Arnold, "SADAFCO," Harvard Business School case study 9-599-021. Boston: Harvard Business School Publishing.

6. Robert E. Kennedy, "Policy Reform, Globalization, and New Opportunities in Emerging Markets," Harvard Business School Working Paper. Boston: Harvard Business School, 2000.

companies rushed into countries such as China, India, and Russia, attracted by their large populations and determined not to miss out on what appeared to be a once-in-a-century opportunity for new sources of revenue growth. At the time, the U.S. administration's export promotion strategy was built around the "Big Emerging Markets Policy," launched in 1994 after the Commerce Department was charged with answering the question, "If we look toward the next century, where will we find the engines of American growth? Which markets hold the most promise?"[7] As already noted, such a rush to investment appears to have been overly optimistic: in an article on the globalization "mistakes of the '90s" that noted that foreign direct investment (FDI) by American companies in East Asia excluding Japan decreased by 74 percent to $1.33 billion between 1997–2000, *Business-Week* commented, "Corporate America doesn't talk much about emerging markets. Things were different a decade ago ... many of these bets fizzled or disappointed."[8]

There is indeed huge long-run potential in international markets, and in emerging markets in particular, but it is poor managerial judgment to confuse long-term potential with short-to-medium term realizable profits—or even revenues. The mismatch between the ambitions of western multinationals and the ability of emerging markets to yield income should be apparent from even a cursory market analysis. More surprising is the fact that most MNCs would not tolerate such loose market analysis in their domestic markets, but they insist on detailed and justified income forecasts based on solid market data. In those cases where a multinational has experienced rapid success in entering emerging markets, it has often been the result of close targeting of specific opportunities:

---

7. United States International Trade Administration, *The Big Emerging Markets: 1996 Outlook and Sourcebook* (Lanham, MD: Bernan Press with the National Technical Information Service, 1996). The "ten big emerging markets" at that time were Mexico, Brazil, Argentina, South Africa, Poland, Turkey, India, South Korea, the ASEAN countries (Indonesia, Thailand, Malaysia, Singapore, and Vietnam), and the Chinese Economic Area (People's Republic of China, Hong Kong, and Taiwan).

8. "Smart Globalization," *BusinessWeek*, August 27, 2001.

Procter & Gamble, for example, has penetrated a range of markets in categories such as shampoo, toothpaste, or paper products such as diapers or feminine protection, moving aggressively to establish first-mover advantage in categories in which their accustomed competitors had yet to enter the mass market in those countries.

This tendency reveals a second major pitfall of foreign market assessment, which is to base entry decisions upon visions or pressures from shareholders or competitors instead of market analysis. Often, much of the foreign overinvestment was made to show shareholders that the firm in which they had invested was aggressive enough in business development, for fear of falling behind competitors who were themselves investing, or through vague notions or "visions" such as the twenty-first century being "the Asian century" as the twentieth century was the American century. The idea that there was a limited window of opportunity was particularly influential, and it created competitive pressures, as exemplified by this statement made by Alex Trotman of Ford: "I can't go down in history as the Ford Chairman who missed China." These arguments are all vulnerable to the fact of market immaturity, even though there are first-mover advantages in some international markets, as discussed later in this chapter. Decades of economic development will be necessary before China or any other emerging market can constitute major profit pools, and in those decades of change there are likely to be opportunities for new entrants to flourish (as many local companies are in fact demonstrating). The fundamentals of market analysis remain as valid in emerging markets as everywhere else—the level of demand and likely market share will depend upon price levels relative to disposable income, competitive intensity, market segmentation patterns, and customer behavior and psychology.

The third major pitfall is to rely upon senior executives' network of contacts as the basis for market selection. In fact, this amounts to abstaining altogether from assessment of candidate markets and substituting entry into a partnership for entry into a market. This method of market selection can take a number of forms, as is evident from the anecdotal history of the internationalization of almost any multinational.

In some cases, a former employee, who decided to return to his or her native country, was given the national exclusive distribution agency. Sometimes, a distributor in one country persuades an MNC to grant distribution in a neighboring country. More simply, many companies agree to persuasive proposals from prospective foreign representatives, who scout trade shows in number once a company makes news in the business media. For example, a prominent U.S.-based leisurewear company entered Italy as its first international market simply because it agreed to a proposal offered by an Italian entrepreneur at a trade fair. In some respects, this is a rational decision—the company had some excess capacity, so the economics looked favorable when costed on a marginal basis, and since the agreement involved the distributor taking title to the goods, the risk was minimal. But the longer-term unforeseen consequences have created difficulties: the Italian distributor positioned the company's brand very differently from its U.S. positioning, as did subsequent European counterparts, which created an international inconsistency with which the firm is still struggling. More generally, many MNCs find that the right distributor for market entry is the wrong partner for long-term market development, and they encounter difficulties in managing the international distributor life cycle (discussed in detail in Chapter 5).

The strongest general support for the network effect is the research on "psychic distance," which demonstrates that companies often select markets that are culturally closest—U.S. companies often enter Canada and the UK before Mexico, for example, while Spanish companies are the major investors in South America.[9] Again, this can be justified as a rational decision, as it minimizes what might be described as the managerial risk of unfamiliarity with the market. But, in the long run, there is no substitute for market analysis and the resultant robust marketing strategies. This will certainly be a sounder basis on which to base a business plan than the level of comfort of the international company's executives.

9. Shawna O'Grady and Henry W. Lane, "The Psychic Distance Paradox," *Journal of International Business Studies*, Vol. 27, No. 2 (1996).

Moreover, although internationalization by minimizing psychic distance is an empirical fact, it should also be noted that many firms from countries without such obvious cultural paths, such as Switzerland or Finland, have internationalized early, extensively, and successfully.

The frequency with which companies make these errors is an example of how lower managerial standards that prevail in domestic marketing are sometimes accepted with regard to international operations. International market entry strategies should be based upon market analysis rather than country analysis, and they should follow a framework that allows for the evolutionary challenge posed by most international markets.

A FRAMEWORK FOR ASSESSING FOREIGN MARKETS

There is no shortage of country information on which to base entry decisions. The problem, from a marketing management perspective, is that it is the wrong sort of information. Specifically, there is a wealth of country-level economic and demographic data available from sources including governments, multinational institutions such as the United Nations or the World Bank, and consulting firms specializing in economic intelligence or risk assessment. These sources of data are valuable from an investment perspective, but they reveal little about the prospects for selling products or services at the operational level of the store or the sales representative. Yet, for two reasons, this information is frequently used for market assessment. First, this country-market data is readily available, whereas product-market information is often difficult or sometimes impossible to obtain.[10] In circumstances in which some product-market

10. Country-market describes the situation when a "market" is defined by national boundaries (e.g., "the French market"), whereas product-market refers to a market defined by products (e.g., "the cosmetics market"). As used in this book, a product-market is a sub-set of a country-market (i.e., product-markets exist within country-markets).

research data is available, often from research organizations that publish market-sizing studies, it is utilized as second-priority information because the multinational intends to alter radically the size and structure of the market. This is connected with the second factor behind this pattern of overestimation of market attractiveness, namely that market entry decisions tend to be taken from an investment perspective by senior executives principally concerned with risk minimization. This information is certainly relevant, but it is incomplete: macroeconomic and national demographic data are often a poor predictor of market opportunity, as the mistakes of the 1990s demonstrate.

The U.S.-based firm Mary Kay Cosmetics (MKC) serves as an illustrative example of this distinction, and it will be used later in this chapter to reinforce the approach described. MKC is a direct marketing company, going to market via a force of independent "beauty consultants" who buy and resell cosmetics and toiletries to contacts either individually or at social gatherings (the "party plan" distribution channel). When considering market entries in Asia, the company arrived at a final decision between Japan and the People's Republic of China (PRC).[11] By the standards of most country-level data, Japan was by far the most attractive: it boasted the highest per capita spend of any country in the world on cosmetics and toiletries, it had high disposable income levels, it already hosted a thriving direct marketing industry, and it had a high proportion of women who did not participate in the workforce. As MKC learned after participating in both markets, however, the market opportunity was far greater in PRC, principally because Chinese women were far more motivated to boost their income by becoming beauty consultants than were their Japanese counterparts. The entrepreneurial opportunity represented by what MKC describes as "the career" (i.e., becoming a beauty consultant) was a far better predictor of how many

---

11. See Nathalie Laidler and John A. Quelch, "Mary Kay Cosmetics: Asian Market Entry," Harvard Business School case study 9-594-023. Boston: Harvard Business School Publishing.

sales could be made than high-level data on incomes and expenditures. In fact, MKC has come to employ a business-specific indicator of market potential within its market assessment framework: the average wage for a female secretary in a country, which can then help the firm estimate the size of the opportunity provided to the average working woman by a career as a beauty consultant.

It is, of course, valuable for inter-country comparisons to be made in terms of GDP, population, regulatory requirements, tariffs, industry size and concentration, and all the other high-level data available. Approaches using this type of information are well established, and they are amply described in other publications.[12] This chapter will focus on digging deeper into marketing-oriented assessments of likely market size and growth prospects. The following simple framework (Figure 2–1) is designed to help international marketing executives ask the right questions when assessing alternative markets.

This framework is based upon analysis at the level of the product-market rather than the country-market, assuming that the dynamics of different industries are at least as different as the characteristics of different countries. In other words, a country that is attractive to one company might be unattractive to another firm because each requires different conditions in order for its business model to thrive. While country analysis might still be useful as a first screen in a hierarchical assessment process (to be followed by more detailed product-market level analysis), it is only at this more local product-specific level that accurate assessment can be realistically attempted. This is a fundamentally different method of market assessment from the prevailing country-level analysis, which is usually based upon macroeconomic or national demographic data. It is based upon two product-market-level concepts:

---

12. See for example the excellent coverage of such analysis in: (1) Warren J. Keegan, *Global Marketing Management*, 7th ed. (Upper Saddle River, NJ: Prentice Hall, 2002); (2) Michael R. Czinkota and Ilkka A. Ronkainen, *International Marketing*, 6th ed. (Forth Worth: Harcourt, 2001).

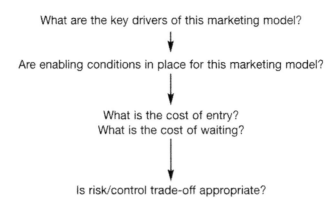

What are the key drivers of this marketing model?

Are enabling conditions in place for this marketing model?

What is the cost of entry?
What is the cost of waiting?

Is risk/control trade-off appropriate?

FIGURE 2–1   The Market Entry Decision—Screening Criteria

MARKETING-MODEL DRIVERS

Different product-markets require different levers for the business to grow, a fact that is self-evidently true to anybody involved in marketing at the operational level. Some markets are brand-sensitive, while others will not grow without intensive distribution or a cadre of technically qualified salespeople. In the example already described, it is a significant insight for Mary Kay to identify that the entrepreneurial opportunity of becoming a beauty consultant is the real driver of its business rather than the overall level of expenditure on toiletries and cosmetics.

ENABLING CONDITIONS

The second core concept is that of enabling conditions—the structural characteristics of the market that are necessary for the marketing model to operate effectively. Only if the enabling conditions are in place will a firm be able to realize its potential. For example, consider a market that is driven by a large number of impulse purchases (such as toys, soft drinks, or ice cream). For marketing to be effective in such product categories, the product has to be available at the moment of impulse, and so an intensive and well-developed distribution system is a prerequisite or an enabling condition. In fact, the lack of such a distribution system is usually identified as the major barrier to market growth in many of the large emerging markets such as China or Russia.

COST OF ENTRY VS. COST OF WAITING

Finally, the cost side of the business equation should be analyzed and weighed against the demand figures already calculated. This has two aspects. First, a company should have a clear idea of the economic costs of participating in the market. This will include questions such as whether local production and/or assembly are required, how many local employees will be required, tariff requirements, and so on. This is another area in which there will be significant differences between product-markets, depending, among other things, upon the bulk-to-value ratio of the products being sold—a lightweight and/or small product, such as a branded pen or an electronic component, incurs far lower transportation costs to import than a high bulk-to-value product such as a disposal bin, which makes the projected income statement for the first few years in the market look more attractive.

To illustrate this approach, consider the hypothetical case of two U.S.-based multinationals considering entry into Vietnam after the U.S. trade embargo was lifted by President Clinton in 1994.[13] "Chemical Corporation" is a specialty chemical company, focusing predominantly on industrial adhesives for use in a wide range of manufacturing applications. "Sports Corporation" markets sportswear and sports-oriented fashion in the footwear and apparel categories, which it traditionally markets through sports-celebrity endorsements. Both companies are global leaders in their industries, and both demand price premiums for their high-quality products (see Table 2–1).

The key driver of Chemical Corporation's marketing model is its sales force. The challenge that members of the sales force face is to convince their key prospective buyers, who are probably

---

13. This section draws upon David J. Arnold and John A. Quelch, "Vietnam: Market Entry Decisions," Harvard Business School case study 9-597-020. Boston: Harvard Business School Publishing.

TABLE 2–1   The Market Entry Decision—Vietnam Example

	KEY DRIVERS OF MARKETING MODEL	ENABLING CONDITIONS	NOTES
CHEMICAL	• Sales personnel • Sophisticated customers	• Management • Relationships	• Low cost-to-serve • Strong local training required • Industrial customers present early
SPORTS	• Brand awareness • Development of sports fashion	• Media • Premium customers • Control of retail	• Strong competitive pressure • Attractive manufacturing base • Niche accessible in cities

engineers, of the value of using chemical fastenings (i.e., adhesives) rather than mechanical fastenings (e.g., nuts and bolts). This is a relatively technical selling challenge, and it requires a professional level of cost/benefit analysis by the customer as well as the salesperson. The enabling condition for Chemical to consider a market attractive, therefore, is the presence of a number of sophisticated manufacturing client companies and the availability of an engineering-trained sales force.

Sports Corporation operates an entirely different model. Its products are aspirational—meaning that the consumer pays the premium not only for product quality, but also for identification with the high-achievement and high-fashion world of the sports stars who endorse it. For such a model to work effectively, therefore, the target market must have a well-developed sports industry, including intensive sports media, and it must also offer opportunities for event sponsorship. In addition, Sports will require a retail sector well developed enough to allow it to control distribution and merchandising, an important factor in maintaining the premium image of image-oriented brands.

Vietnam in the late 1990s looks like two different places from the perspective of these two companies. It is an attractive market for Chemical Corporation because of two critical factors. First, the enabling conditions are present at an acceptable level. The sophisticated manufacturing clients that it seeks are largely multinational firms rather than local Vietnamese concerns, and as soon as the trade embargo was lifted, a number of American firms joined the European and Asian companies that had already been attracted by Vietnam as a manufacturing base. Moreover, there was a pool of recently trained American engineering graduates who could be recruited as sales personnel—these were mostly second-generation members of the Vietnamese diaspora, originally displaced to the United States by the Vietnam War and now seeking to return to their ancestral home. The second critical factor that renders Vietnam attractive to Chemical is the low cost-to-serve. Adhesives are not bulky products, and they can affordably be exported from existing production locations in Asia, obviating the need for Chemical to establish local manufacturing.

The situation facing Sports Corporation is quite different on both counts. First, the enabling conditions are largely absent: whereas a cluster of manufacturing firms can establish their operations within a year or two of a market being opened, it takes several years or even decades for a previously communist society to adopt a western-style affinity for sports and for the attendant media, events, and retail sectors to develop. In addition, the income levels necessary to afford the premium prices of Sports Corporation's products will also take decades to spread to a critical mass of the population. In fact, the strongest attraction of Vietnam to Sports may be as a manufacturing base for reexporting rather than as a revenue-generating market. Whereas there is latent demand for Chemical's products in Vietnam, Sports faces a market in which neither latent demand nor enabling conditions are present, given its marketing model.

This method of analyzing markets can be characterized as "bottom-up" rather than "top-down," as it is based upon product-market data that is then scaled up into a forecast of market feasibility rather than starting from high-level country data and attempting to dig down to product-market forecasts. This approach will also be used to illustrate the forecasting of market size. Firstly, however, it is important to consider the type of data required for such an approach.

GUIDELINES FOR MARKET RESEARCH IN ASSESSING INTERNATIONAL MARKETS

One of the reasons market assessment is so challenging is that it often takes place in a data vacuum. In many countries, especially those usually categorized as "emerging markets," market research is either simply not available or not feasible (most often in terms of cost). This might be because of a lack of the infrastructure necessary for market research, such as telephones or trained interviewers, or because customers simply lack any experience in the product category. Almost always, it is impossible to recruit a sample that is even close to representative of the target market population. This explains the lack of analysis underpinning many entry strategies and the reliance on published country data. However, experienced international marketing executives learn that there are ways of getting closer to the market data required to support a more rigorous and close-up analysis. The three key issues are the type of intermediary used for data gathering, the type of data gathered, and the use of analogous markets for estimation purposes.

First, the lack of market research firms with trained professionals should not justify a resignation to a lack of primary research. A number of other types of intermediary are nearly always available. A frequent first option is to turn to professional service firms such as accountants, management consultancies, or lawyers. Many of these types of organizations have internationalized early, have offices in nearly all countries, and have connections in local business communities. An internationalizing firm can often contact an office of a firm with which it has an existing corporate relationship for help in market research. A second option is to turn to local universities:

students, especially business students, are usually eager to undertake research projects, especially for international firms and particularly if such projects can be incorporated into their coursework for credit. A third option is that an international firm with existing subsidiaries or distributors in the region could turn to those units for research help and request a suitable executive to undertake the necessary research, including time spent in the target market.

Such sources may of course lack the training required to produce market research of a high professional validity and rigor, but experienced MNCs increasingly will use such intermediaries, and other types of ad-hoc agents may present themselves opportunistically. At the least, basic errors of misunderstanding about country-markets can be avoided by undertaking such research, and the essentials of a marketing plan, such as likely price levels and the extent of distribution networks, can usually be ascertained. In such projects, it is critical to have a local presence—somebody who has the contacts necessary to recruit researchers and can supervise those gathering data. Any of the three categories of intermediary described (e.g., a distributor in a neighboring country, a partner in a local professional services firm, or a local university professor) could potentially provide such a contact. The key principle is to use local researchers so that research can be executed close up to the market (e.g., in the local language and in line with local culture) and so that basic misunderstandings are avoided.

The second key issue is the type of data gathered. This will obviously vary according to product-market characteristics, and it may be constrained by local marketing and communications infrastructure. In the case of assessing Vietnam, for example, Chemical would need to know the number of trained engineers employed as buyers for manufacturing firms, while Sports would face the much more difficult challenge of measuring awareness of major sports stars. While acknowledging such situational considerations, it is still possible to make a few generalizations that apply to all situations:

- It is important to use multiple indicators. Reliance on a single measure for an estimate of market potential is certainly less reliable than use of multiple measures from which a conclusion can be triangulated. Experienced MNCs have assessment models that include perhaps a dozen or more key indicators of market dynamics that can be applied across any combination of country-markets.

- A company should develop customized indicators, which are specific to its own product-market and which have previously proven useful in predicting potential. A good example is Mary Kay Cosmetics' use of the average wage of a female secretary as a basis for estimating the potential earnings improvement for women who become beauty consultants—this information would be of little relevance to most other companies. Such company-specific indicators would clearly have to be based upon intelligent interpretation of previous experience in international markets.

- Never assess markets in isolation, but always conduct comparative assessments of multiple markets, even if the markets have little in common. Just as triangulation is an effective strategy for reducing uncertainty with regard to measures of market potential, so comparative assessment of markets will reveal questions that executives never discern when examining individual markets. This recognizes the fact that absolute measurement of market potential is impossible, thus increasing the value of a portfolio approach in which alternative priorities are considered.

- Favor observations of behavior, such as purchasing patterns or descriptions of distribution networks, over reports of opinion, such as likelihood to purchase or price sensitivity. This approach, always valuable, is particularly important in international markets in which accurate surveys of customer perceptions are often impossible. Customers are notoriously unreliable predictors of their reaction to new products or other future market developments. Reports of behavioral patterns in the marketplace offer at least a basis for intermarket comparison, and they are usually also a sound basis for marketing planning when compared with opinion surveys. Because the product-market being researched is often underdeveloped or embryonic, it may be necessary to include in the research a brief measurement of behavior with regard to substitute products (for example, the consumption of tea, buttermilk, or any other relevant nonalcoholic beverage might be a useful market indicator for a soft drinks firm).

It is also important to take a flexible approach to the type of data gathered, recognizing that a variety of wider contextual factors may influence market activity in different countries. In Mediterranean countries, for example, a package delivery service could not schedule its usual 5 P.M. or 6 P.M. final pick-up, given the practice of an afternoon break followed by offices opening until perhaps 7 P.M. or 8 P.M. Similarly, products that women buy in supermarkets in the western markets would probably underperform in conservative Muslim countries such as Saudi Arabia since most women do not drive or shop alone and therefore seldom visit supermarkets. An expanded view of the contextual distance between countries is necessary, and a useful framework for understanding the types of issues to look for is provided by Pankaj Ghemawat in a paper entitled "Distance Still Matters: The Hard Reality of Global Expansion."[14] Basing his analysis upon the high failure rates of foreign market entries in terms of meeting performance objectives, Ghemawat argues that even in a world in which telecommunications and other technologies appear to be reducing the importance of distance, there remain significant country-specific barriers to entry that constitute the "distance" involved in entering the market from outside. His CAGE framework identifies the cultural, administrative, geographic, and economic sources of intercountry distance, and provides guidelines on which

---

14. Pankaj Ghemawat, "Distance Still Matters: The Hard Reality of Global Expansion," *Harvard Business Review* (September 2001): 3–11.

product-markets would be more affected by each. For example, cultural barriers such as different languages or social norms would be a significant source of inter-country distance for culturally-sensitive products such as television or movies; administrative barriers such as lower levels of intergovernmental cooperation will impact markets with high levels of regulation, such as aerospace, healthcare, or pharmaceuticals. It is worth noting that even in the movie or TV industry, in which U.S. firms and their products enjoy a global dominance, research shows that one of the key differentiators between the winners and losers in emerging markets is their willingness to localize their content, In China, for example, the customization practiced by STAR TV and MTV has given the companies an advantage over less adaptable rivals such as Time Warner.[15]

The third key approach in foreign market assessment is the use of "parallel" markets to forecast potential by analogy. When faced with a lack of data from a candidate market, experienced MNCs will use a number of surrogate measures from comparable markets as the basis for a market assessment. These might include data on a comparable product in the same country; the same product in a comparable country, the same product with a neighboring distributor, or a competitor or comparable company in the same country. The more data points that can be obtained, the better the internationalizing firm can triangulate and so reduce the uncertainty in its estimate of market potential. Figure 2–2 illustrates a number of ways in which estimates may be produced using this approach. For example, if a firm is estimating market potential in Argentina, and it knows that it already sells $10 million in Brazil, it might initially estimate the potential at Argentina at $2.3 million based upon the relative size of the two countries' populations, and it may then double this to $4.6 million to adjust for higher average disposable incomes in Argentina. Alternatively, Firm A may know that it sells 50 percent as much as its competitor,

15. Lyn Baranowski, Nitin Nayar, Sheeba Philip, "Breaking New Ground: Foreign Media Companies Enter the Chinese Cable TV Market," Student Field Research Paper, Harvard Business School, December 2002.

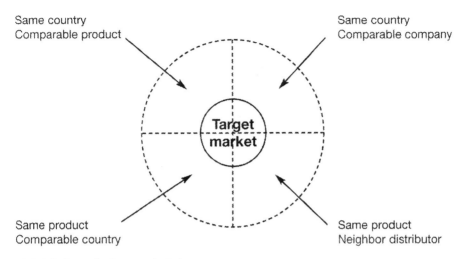

Same country
Comparable product

Same country
Comparable company

Target market

Same product
Comparable country

Same product
Neighbor distributor

FIGURE 2–2 Market Forecasting by Analogy

Firm B, in Brazil, and it knows that Firm B sells $10 million in Argentina, so it estimates its potential there at $5 million. These forms of extrapolation should definitely be regarded as a fallback position, and any form of direct data from the market in question are preferable to this form of estimation. However, situations do occur when this is the best information available. Moreover, it can always be useful to conduct this type of estimation exercise, even when direct market data is available, as an additional insight into likely market sales levels.

FORECASTING MARKET POTENTIAL

Forecasting market sales levels remains an exercise in the art of estimation rather than the science of marketing, and even after years of international marketing experience, the difficulty of this challenge explains many of the managerial errors in market entry strategy that have been observed. However, it is significant that in almost all cases, the error is in one direction—namely, an overestimation of market potential. This may be because other pressures, such as competitor entries or shareholder pressures for aggressive investment, are driving market expansion strategies, and without robust market data, a firm errs on the side of optimism in its forecasts. The key approach to really reading a market is to start at the demand level rather than the aggregate level of country macroeconomic or demographic data, a distinction previously described as bottom-up as contrasted with top-down. These approaches will now be illustrated using data from the case study on the entry of Mary Kay Cosmetics into China.

TOP-DOWN FORECASTING

The typical method of market assessment can be described as "top-down" because it is based upon country-level variables, and the data are then reduced to arrive at an estimate of sales. The progression is therefore from country data to product-level data. The two most commonly employed categories of indicator are macroeconomic and population data because both are readily available for almost any country. If a country's GNP is known, for example, market size can be estimated by calculating the proportion of the population likely to have the necessary disposable income to buy the relevant product. Similarly, if the population is known, estimates can be made of the size of the relevant demographic segment (e.g., men aged 18–40). In some cases, one of these indicators can be used alone to produce a simple market forecast. For example, a company might know, from experience in other international markets, that there is a correlation between GNP and market size and that a GNP of x therefore supports a market forecast of y. More frequently, however, the national data is processed via a series of assumptions about the proportion of the economy or the population that will constitute the market. An example of this will follow. The final assumption, of course, will be to estimate the share of the market that the company will be able to achieve.

In principle, this is a perfectly good method of market assessment or forecasting because the variables are certainly relevant to market size. In practice, however, this method tends to produce inaccurate forecasts, and in particular it is responsible for overestimates of market size because macroeconomic and population data provide a good indication of market *potential,* but no indication of the likelihood of potential customers (or "prospects" as salespeople call them) being converted into actual customers. The existence or availability of a certain number of prospects is certainly relevant to market plans, but a more fine-grained view of marketplace dynamics is necessary to arrive at realistic estimates of market revenues. Interestingly, many Internet businesses foundered after it was realized that "eyeballs," or website traffic, was in fact only market potential.

As an illustration of this method of forecasting, Table 2–2 shows how Mary Kay Cosmetics might forecast market potential in China and, more specifically, in Shanghai province. This shows the typical "Dutch auction" process that such an approach entails (i.e., we start with an unrealistically high figure that is repeatedly reduced to arrive eventually at the forecast). Starting with the total population, a series of assumptions are made to adjust a limited set of known facts: 50 percent of the population is accessible nationally, but all in Shanghai province; 50 percent is female; 33 percent of females are in the right age group; a certain proportion (higher in Shanghai province) have the necessary disposable income; a certain proportion of the income will be spent on cosmetics and toiletries; and MKC can achieve a certain market share.

None of the assumptions is irrational, and it should be noted that this top-down forecast is working with some product-level data and not just national macroeconomic and demographic figures. Nevertheless, the resultant forecast is far higher than proved to be realistic and far higher than the bottom-up forecast discussed in the next section. This is because the forecast is produced using assumptions taken from static and established structures within markets and economies, and it completely fails to address the challenge of the change required before Chinese women purchase cosmetics and toiletries at these rates.

TABLE 2–2   Top-Down Market Forecasting: Mary Kay in China

	NOTE	COUNTRY	SHANGHAI
TOTAL POPULATION		1.3 bn	60 mm
ACCESSIBLE	50% (80% E, 30% urban)	650 mm	60 mm
FEMALE	50%	325 mm	30 mm
AGE 18–35	33%	110 mm	10 mm
DISPOSABLE INCOME	41 mm > $18K = 4% Assume 15% > $10K Assume 20% in Shanghai	17 mm	2 mm
PER CAPITA SPEND	Shanghai: $120 × 75% × 30%/mo. Country: Japan = $400 Assume twice GDP ratio	$45	$320
MARKET VALUE P/A		$765 mm	$640 mm
MKC SHARE @ 5%		$38 mm	$16 mm

Estimates are for country and for Shanghai province.

1. It is known that 80 percent of the Chinese population live in the east and 30 percent in urban areas, which makes those portions of the population more accessible. It is assumed that all Shanghai province is accessible.

2. It is known that 41 million households have disposable income above $18,000 per annum, and it is estimated that significant expenditure on cosmetics and toiletries begins at $10,000.

3. Research indicates that the typical consumer in Shanghai has $120 disposable income per month, of which 75 percent is spent on essential items (e.g., housing and food), of which 30 percent is spent on cosmetics and toiletries, resulting in potential spending of $27 per month and equaling $320 per year. It is known that the equivalent figure for Japan is $400 and that Japan's GDP is some 20 times larger than China's. It is assumed that Chinese women spend twice as much of their disposable income on cosmetics than Japanese women do.

BOTTOM-UP FORECASTING

By contrast, Table 2–3 shows a bottom-up forecast for Shanghai province. The restriction to the most prosperous province of the country in itself constitutes a more realistic starting point. More fundamentally, this forecast adopts an entirely different approach, starting from MKC's customized indicator and building up to an answer to the question, What level of business would be required to offer secretaries the opportunity to increase their wage by 50 percent by becoming a Mary Kay beauty consultant? This quantifies the opportunity at an individual level, and it is assumed that the number of women for whom this opportunity is valid can then be estimated.

Some of the assumptions here are more robust because they are within the control of the company (e.g., the assumption that beauty consultants would have a revenue of $4.50 per unit, representing a 50 percent margin, is based upon company costs and pricing decisions). This forecast also makes a number of other assumptions already seen in the top-down forecast (for example, that women in the target age and income group spend on average $324 annually on cosmetics and toiletries and that MKC can achieve a 5 percent market share), but it employs them quite differently. In this case, the conservative assumption is made that all the expenditure is on items at the MKC price level of $9, even though this is at the higher-priced end of the market.

This forecast produces an estimated market potential of $324 million, compared with $640 million in the previous top-down forecast. This reflects the quite different approach taken—put simplistically, it is based on answering a "What is required to achieve *x*?" question rather than a "How large might the market be?" question. The task to be achieved, a 50 percent increase in income for the average secretary who

TABLE 2–3 Bottom-Up Market Forecasting: Mary Kay in Shanghai

	ASSUME IMPROVED AVERAGE FEMALE WAGE BY 50%	
CURRENT WAGE	$125 × 12	$1,500
TARGET WAGE	NB: In Taiwan, average consultant wage is $3,000	$2,250
@ $4.50/ UNIT, TARGET =		500 units
AVERAGE CUSTOMER SPENDING =	$27 × 12	$324
@ 9/UNIT, TARGET =		36 units
= $3/MONTH	= *unrealistic!*	

ASSUME 3 MKC UNITS/MONTH @ $9 = 50% OF WALLET

scales up to annual cosmetics spending	$648
scales up to annual disposable income	$2,880

SHANGHAI TARGET POPULATION =

if 2mm H/Hs > $10,000, women @ $2,880 =	2mm
annual spending @ $13.50/month	$324mm
MKC share @ 5%	$16.2mm
number of consultants @ $2,250	7,200

1. *Assume that the Mary Kay opportunity is attractive if it can increase the average female wage in Shanghai by 50 percent to $2,250. Note that this is high, as the average wage in Taiwan is $3,000, and Taiwan has much higher levels of GDP and disposable income.*
2. *To earn $2,250, a consultant must sell 500 units (@ $4.50 gross margin per unit). However, at the average consumer price of $9, this would consume all the cosmetics budget of the average earner for only three units per month or 36 units per year. This is regarded as unrealistic.*
3. *Alternatively, assume that a consumer purchases three Mary Kay units per month, and that this represents 50 percent of cosmetics spending. This scales up to an annual cosmetics spending of $648 per year and (using the income structure from Table 2–2) an annual disposable income of some $3,000 (about twice the average female wage).*
4. *We know that there are about 2 million households in Shanghai province with disposable income of $10,000, so assume this equates to individual women at $3,000. Assuming 5 percent market capture again, we can expect 100,000 customers, or a market size of $16.2 million, which would support 7,200 consultants at the higher earnings level.*

becomes a beauty consultant, is specific to the company and based on experience in other markets. It is quite typical that a realistic bottom-up forecast would produce an estimate of market potential much lower (in this case, 50 percent lower) than a "top-down forecast." Such an approach, using benchmarks or hurdle rates, is commonplace in investment projects, but it is rarely used in international market assessments. In this case, the bottom-up forecast proved to be more accurate. In fact, sales were below the projected level in the first year, but they exceeded all forecasts after a few years in the market. Because the company had planned conservatively, based upon a realistic and market-driven forecast, it has been able to build a successful business in China without falling prey to initial overestimation of sales potential and the challenge of building the business.

FIRST-MOVER ADVANTAGE

Besides the estimation of market potential, the other major decision in market entry strategy is that of the timing of entry. This, too, has assumed great prominence in the international boom of the 1990s because so many entries, especially in emerging markets, were justified on the grounds of an urgent need to participate in the market early. Whereas the early internationalization of many firms was opportunistic and incremental, this wave of global expansion of the 1990s was characterized by a certain urgency, as if there existed limited windows of opportunity that would reward only those players bold enough to move early. Indeed, companies frequently acknowledged that any reasonable sales forecast would not estimate profitability for years to come, but they nonetheless entered the market because of a belief in the concept of first-mover advantage (sometimes referred to as pioneer advantage), one of the most widely established theories of business in the minds of executives and investors alike.

According to this theory, the first entrant in a new market enjoys a unique advantage that later competitors cannot overcome (i.e., the advantage is somehow structural, and therefore sustainable). For some companies, this reasoning is validated by history. Procter & Gamble, for example, has always trailed rivals such as Unilever in certain large markets including India and some Latin American countries, and the most obvious explanation is that its European rivals were participating in these countries long before it, simply for reasons of European colonial history. Given that history, it is reasonable for Procter & Gamble to err on the side of urgency in reaction to the opening of large markets such as Russia or China.

For many companies, however, the concept of pioneer advantage was little more than an article of faith, and it was applied to country-market entry, to product-market entry, and, in particular, to the "new economy" opportunities created by the Internet. Although the "get big quick" philosophy of the dot-com boom has been rather discredited by the subsequent dot-com bust, the "get in early" philosophy of pioneer advantage remains largely accepted. To some extent, this is correct: the advantages gained by European companies from being early in "colonial" markets provide some evidence of pioneer advantage. Moreover, as will be argued later, there are a number of sources of pioneer advantage that are more likely to be present in emerging economies. Nevertheless, it should be emphasized that first-mover advantage is overrated as a managerial rule of thumb. Indeed, in many situations, there may be disadvantages to being first. These can be of two types. First, at a more general level, the absence of any pioneer advantage results in poor business performance, caused by a lack of return on the investment required for market entry. This is what has happened to many western MNCs who rushed into Russia and China in the early 1990s and a few years later were attempting to stem their losses. Second, and more specifically, there is the danger that a pioneer will not be able to recoup the investment made in marketing required to kick-start a new market.[16] In such cases, it may well transpire that a "fast follower" can benefit from the market development

---

16. For a more detailed discussion, see Gerard J. Tellis, Peter N. Golder, and Clayton M. Christensen, *Will and Vision: How Latecomers Grow to Dominate Markets* (McGraw Hill, 2001).

investments of the first mover and, without those pioneering costs, leapfrog into earlier profitability.

An example of this is provided by Sony's attempts to develop and dominate the market for car navigation systems.[17] As a result of considerable investment in both product technology and marketing, Sony was the market leader in this category in 1993, at which time some 80 percent of worldwide unit sales were in Japan. However, the drivers of demand in Japan (a widespread love of technology, a complex and relatively poorly signposted road system, and extensive use of cars for leisure driving well away from the home) were not present to the same extent in North America and Western Europe. In those markets, large investments in marketing would be required to persuade customers that they needed an expensive technological addition to their car to replace a cheap paper roadmap. Moreover, product adaptations were required: Europeans needed multilanguage capabilities, and Americans, more concerned with traffic congestion than with directions, required links to live traffic information services. As a committed pioneer, these up-front costs would have to be carried by Sony, but there was nothing to stop later entrants from free-riding on this market development investment and picking up customers. In fact, later entrants completely outflanked Sony in Europe and America by going to market via the OEM channel instead of addressing consumers directly via the auto aftermarket, as had been the case in Japan.[18] It seems likely that later entrants benefited from Sony's market development investment, but they found an even better way of getting consumers to consider navigation systems: by allowing them to try them out in test drives or rental cars. As early as 1995,

---

17. Yoshinori Fujikawa and John A. Quelch, "Sony Corporation: Car Navigation Systems," Harvard Business School case study 9-597-032. Boston: Harvard Business School Publishing.

18. OEM stands for original equipment manufacturer. In this case, it refers to automobile manufacturers offering navigation systems as optional extras on new cars or including them in cars in rental fleets. The aftermarket is a retail channel in which car owners buy accessories for their car after purchase.

Sony's market share was in decline even in Japan, and it remains well behind the leaders.

This ability of later entrants to free-ride on the pioneer's market development investment is the most common source of first-mover disadvantage, and it offers insight into the two conditions necessary for first-mover advantage to accrue. Understanding these two conditions is essential for a critical understanding of the market entry situation, and it should inform all such decisions. For first-mover advantage to exist, the following two conditions must apply:

- First, there must be a scarce resource in the market that the entrant company can acquire.
- Second, the entrant company must be able to tie in that scarce resource so that it is not available to competitors.

If there is no scarce marketing resource, then it is clear that later entrants have full and equal access to the market and that, conversely, the pioneer has no advantage. For example, consider the widely held opinion that the first brand in the market can have the advantage of establishing the standard in its category and become the generic example of the product (like "Band Aid" or "Hoover"). In such cases, the scarce resource is at the front of the consumer's mind—or an established position in the limited attention or memory the consumer is prepared to devote to this category. In the case of car navigation systems, this appears not to have happened, and consumers did not regard the pioneer products as the gold standard. Alternatively, consider the role of government in markets in which it is necessary for foreign firms to obtain a permit or license to sell their products. In such cases, the license, and perhaps government approval more generally, may be a scarce resource that will not be granted to all comers.

The second condition is also necessary for first-mover advantage to develop—and for the same reason. The most common supposed source of first-mover advantage, brand preference from being the first brand known, is based on the idea that brand attitudes are unlikely to change once established. In fact, a long stream of research has failed to establish conclusively the existence of this phenomenon, and it is clear that in many cases, consumers consider the alternatives available at the time of their first purchase. In other cases, such as contracts with distributors or other partners, it is clear that the advantage can be expected to last years rather than months, so it might provide a sustained competitive advantage.

SOURCES OF FIRST-MOVER ADVANTAGE IN EMERGING MARKETS

Having emphasized the need for caution and rigor in thinking about first-mover advantage, it should be noted that there are a number of potential sources of advantage, relating to structural aspects of the market or country, that are *more likely* to accrue in international markets than in the domestic situation. In particular, these structural factors are more likely to be present in emerging markets because in such less-developed markets, more resources are likely to be scarce.[19]

GOVERNMENT RELATIONS

National and local governments, and other regulatory bodies are far more influential in emerging markets (EMs) than in developed-country market systems. This reflects both the recent history of many emerging-market countries as command economies or closed markets and the desire of many host governments to build local business as the economy grows and FDI inflows increase, rather than allowing foreign firms to capture all the growth. On a more operational level, it also reflects the importance of government-led infrastructure projects in the early stages of development. The early establishment of relationships with government can result in tangible benefits such as the granting of one of a limited number of licenses or permits; China, for example, has decided to restrict the number of western MNCs to which it gives joint venture

---

19. David J. Arnold and John A. Quelch, "New Strategies in Emerging Markets," *Sloan Management Review*, Vol. 40, No. 1 (Fall 1998).

permits in many industries. In addition, many EM governments are still in the process of establishing a new pro-business regulatory framework for their countries, and MNCs already investing in an EM will clearly be favorably positioned to influence the regulation of the market in areas such as price control or the opening of communications media suitable for their promotional activities. On a more general level, early market entry may also demonstrate a commitment to an emerging market that wins longer-term government favor. Executives familiar with EMs invariably stress the greater importance of personal relationships with key local players (in both the public and private sectors), and MNCs that have participated longer in EMs can be expected to enjoy stronger and more favorable relationships than later entrants. First entrants also get access to the best government-nominated local joint-venture partners.

PENT-UP DEMAND

A substantial reservoir of pent-up demand for previously unavailable but known western brands may exist in EMs, offering a platform level of sales not available in the new product-market spaces assumed by most models of first-mover advantage. In former command economies, surplus (i.e., unsatisfied) demand had prevailed for many years in a "seller's market" in which choice was so restricted that cash was not spent.[20] In addition, customers may already have been aware of the product, even though it was previously unavailable in their country, via international travel, international media, or informal channels. In many cases, therefore, conditions may be different from those encountered in the introductory stages of product life cycles in developed markets, where slow diffusion of product awareness and familiarity often result in slow sales take-off after launch. The distinctive conditions of EMs provide first entrants with a nonrecurring beachhead of sales, which can be expected to provide medium-term advantages through repeat purchase.

---

20. Avraham Shama, "Transforming the Consumer in Russia and Eastern Europe," *International Marketing Review*, Vol. 9, No. 2 (1992): 43–59.

MARKETING PRODUCTIVITY

The low cost base of EMs has long been recognized in production location decisions, but it is also relevant to the timing of market entry. In this case, the relevant comparison is not only with global costs, but also with future costs. Low advertising rates per capita in EMs enable brands to be launched and brand awareness to be built very economically. Advertising rates increase rapidly with economic development; for example, they increased ten-fold in real terms in Poland within five years of the fall of communism. Lower levels of competitive spending in EMs can also mean that marketing investments produce higher levels of awareness, share of voice (the proportion of total promotion in the market accounted for by one firm or brand), or shelf space.

MARKETING RESOURCES

While an undeveloped marketing infrastructure is frequently used to justify delaying entry, it can also be seen as a plus. Resources such as distribution channels or media access are often more scarce in EMs. Although the number of managers with both emerging market and international experience is growing, it remains a constraint and thus a potential source of advantage to MNCs that have entered multiple EMs and have therefore developed an internal pool of managers with EM experience. This is a difference of degree rather than of kind; the preemptive advantage accruing from such factors is recognized in first-mover advantage research, but the effect is qualitatively more significant in EMs.

LEARNING

EMs often demand and certainly provide opportunities for innovation in marketing or operations, and the consequent learning can be transferred to other markets. It is widely recognized that the differential ability of MNCs to leverage leading-edge ideas and best practices across operating subsidiaries, in marketing and other functional areas, can be a critical source of competitive advantage.[21] For example, the absence of developed distribution infrastructures in many EMs has prompted MNCs to create innovative distribution processes or more robust product packaging that can prove transferable to developed markets. The scale of many EMs also offers opportunities: fast-food chain Kentucky Fried Chicken (KFC) is pioneering its largest restaurants in China. These restaurants are, on average, twice the size of outlets in the United States due to the greater emphasis on eat-in rather than take-out patronage. KFC's understanding, developed in EMs, of how to run large-scale outlets may be transferable to developed markets. Such "reverse learning" from emerging to developed markets, which can be driven by either the need to adapt to unique market conditions or by "second-time around" learning from previous mistakes, can give emerging-market pioneers a competitive advantage. Also important is the leverage possible from early development of a capability in managing emerging market operating units— given the steep learning curve facing MNCs and the fact that most feel obliged by competitive pressures to enter a series of EMs in quick succession.

SUMMARY

Assessment of foreign markets and estimation of international market potential constitute significant challenges that many internationalizing firms have failed to meet. It is critical that senior executives base their assessment on close analysis of a product-market rather than more general economic and demographic country data. Key points covered in this chapter include the following:

- The importance of forecasting demand as possible sales in a 3–5-year timeframe (as appropriate for the firm's

---

21. Warren J. Keegan, *Global Marketing Management*, 5th ed. (Englewood Cliffs, NJ: Prentice Hall, 1995); Christopher A. Bartlett and Sumantra Ghoshal, *Managing Across Borders* (Boston: Harvard Business School Press, 1989).

planning cycle) rather than total long-run potential sales. This is one area of management in which a solely long-term focus can destroy value.

- The importance of gathering data at the product-market level rather than purely at the country level. The same country-market looks very different through the lens of different industries.

- The concepts of market drivers (the most influential elements of the marketing program) and enabling conditions (the critical success factors for that model). Again, these will differ significantly by industry.

- The importance of customized indicators for each firm; for example, the relevance of the average female secretarial wage for Mary Kay Cosmetics. Such indicators should be part of a multifactor database used for assessing market attractiveness.

- The value of a market-based "bottom-up" sales forecast rather than a country-level "top-down" forecast. The former is usually more conservative and more accurate.

- A rigorous definition of first-mover advantage: it requires sustainable appropriation of a scarce marketing resource rather than simply an early entry. The scarcity of some marketing resources in emerging markets in particular make first-mover advantage a real possibility.

3 STRATEGIES FOR ENTERING AND DEVELOPING INTERNATIONAL MARKETS

The process of penetrating and then developing an international market is a difficult one, which many companies still identify as an Achilles' heel in their global capabilities. In fundamental terms, entering a new country-market is very like a start-up situation, with no sales, no marketing infrastructure in place, and little or no knowledge of the market. Despite this, companies usually treat this situation as if it were an extension of their business, a source of incremental revenues for existing products and services. Two aspects of the typical approach are particularly striking. First, companies often pursue this new business opportunity with a focus on minimizing risk and investment— the complete opposite of the approach usually advocated for genuine start-up situations. Second, from a marketing perspective, many companies break the founding principle of marketing—that a firm should start by analyzing the market, and then, and only then, decide on its offer in terms of products, services, and marketing programs. In fact, it is far more common to see international markets as opportunities to increase sales of existing products and so to adopt a "sales push" rather than a market-driven approach. Given this overall approach, it is not surprising that performance is often disappointing. As was discussed in Chapter 1, profitability in international markets has lagged behind average firm profitability for much of the last two decades (the "foreign investment profitability gap"). This may well be because of what Ghemawat and Ghadar describe as "top-line obsession," a focus on revenue growth rather than profitability growth.[1] The link between this perspective and a view of international sales as incremental business is self-evident. And, after all, many firms enter new country-markets through the indirect channel of a local independent distributor or agent, in which case the multinationals will not know their costs and therefore their operating profitability in the markets. Although more mature firms are altering the way they enter and penetrate new international markets, the mixed results in the post-2001 recession demonstrate that this remains a challenging phase of internationalization.

This common mismatch between expectations and situational requirements stems, above all, from a failure to follow in international operations the marketing strategy process that is probably established in the core domestic business. This may be because participation in the market is indirect (i.e., via an independent local distributor or agent, rather than via a directly controlled marketing subsidiary). It also often reflects a lack of control over strategic marketing and a failure to think rigorously about how the business will develop over the course of several years. While it is true that certain distinctive characteristics of an international marketing situation demand a different approach to marketing, this is not a reason for standards of strategic marketing management to be relaxed. This chapter will begin by examining these unique international marketing challenges and then discuss, in turn, several phases of the process of market entry and development, including the following:

- The objectives of market entry, which will have implications for the strategy and organization adopted.
- The choice of market entry mode (i.e., the form of marketing organization through which the company participates in the market). Particular attention will be paid to the low-intensity modes of entry most commonly favored in market entry situations.

---

1. Pankaj Ghemawat and Fariboz Ghadar, "The Dubious Logic of Global Megamergers," *Harvard Business Review*, July–August 2000.

- The marketing entry strategy, with a particular focus on the lessons learned from the strategies of western multinationals in emerging markets.
- A framework for the overall evolution of an international marketing strategy.

WHAT IS DIFFERENT ABOUT INTERNATIONAL MARKETING?

Most executives are quite clear that international marketing is different from home-country marketing, and most multinational companies insist that their senior managers have international experience on their resumés. Despite this pragmatic recognition of the uniqueness of the international marketplace, there has been little agreement over the exact nature of this distinctiveness. Although the question has been long and inconclusively discussed by academics and business analysts, agreement has been limited to the valid but rather obvious observation that international marketing, as opposed to marketing in a single country, takes place in an environment of increased complexity and uncertainty, in areas as varied as consumer behavior and government regulation. This suggests that the differences between domestic and international marketing are differences of degree rather than underlying differences of kind. In fact, there are certain distinctive characteristics in international operations that, while they may not establish international marketing as a separate theoretical subdomain of marketing, nevertheless have a great bearing on managerial decisions. They are:

A CONTEXT OF RAPID BUSINESS GROWTH AND ORGANIZATIONAL LEARNING

Penetration of a foreign market is a zero-base process. At the point of market entry, the foreign entrant has no existing business and little or no market knowledge, particularly with regard to the managerial competence necessary to operate in the new market environment. During the years after market entry, therefore, the rate of change in the country-specific marketing capability of the firm is likely to be greater than the rate of change in the market environment, and firm effects may dominate market effects in shaping strategy. This is particularly important given the business context, in which the generation of new business is of prime importance—rather than efficiency in managing a relatively stable business. This usually results in (a) entering the market via a partnership with a local distributor or other marketing agent rather than via a directly controlled marketing unit and (b) a relatively rapid sequence of changes to the marketing strategy (such as new product introductions or expansion of distribution) or to the marketing organization (e.g., taking over marketing responsibility from the local distributor).

THE HIERARCHICAL NATURE OF DECISIONS

International market situations are multilevel in their decision focus, with a hierarchy of decisions from country assessment and performance measurement decisions through to more traditional marketing mix allocations and programs. Thus, an executive responsible for a country in which the firm participates only for revenue generation and not for production (a common situation) is simultaneously managing country-level trends in the economy or government, and marketing decisions such as the product range or price level. In the domestic market, by contrast, these decision levels are addressed by separate specialists.

MANAGING A MULTIMARKET NETWORK

From the time a company enters its second country-market, it will inevitably be influenced by its previous experience. The greater the number of national markets in which a company participates, the more likely it is to seek to manage them as an aggregated network rather than as independent units. Marketing strategy decisions in one country-market may in this case be made against extra-market criteria. For example, price levels may be set to minimize the difference among markets and to maintain a price corridor rather than purely to reflect local market conditions. Similarly, a multinational company may subsidize price levels in one market for strategic reasons while recouping that loss in another market. This ability to leverage a global network is sometimes described as "the global chess game,"[2] and it is increasingly regarded as one of the key advantages enjoyed by a global firm relative to local players, partly because of the increasing globalization of firms and their consequent opportunities to integrate national operations. In practice, this frequently results in asymmetric competition in any single market, with different companies pursuing different objectives and setting different performance standards. As discussed later in this chapter, it is possible that one company may be participating in the market simply to learn, and it may therefore tolerate low profitability, while others are pursuing more conventional profit maximization goals.

CO-LOCATION OF STRATEGIC MARKETING AND DISTRIBUTION FUNCTIONS

A national distribution channel for an international corporation is usually responsible not just for the traditional distribution functions,[3] but it is the *de facto* branch of the company in that country with an exclusive agency for the territory and responsibility for marketing strategy. The distribution unit in the country-market, whether an independent organization or a wholly-owned subsidiary, has to manage a strategy for growth, and it will therefore be judged on organizational criteria including feasibility, level of desired risk, supportability, and control issues. By contrast, distribution management in domestic markets is largely concerned with the implementation of preexisting marketing strategies such as communication platforms and target

---

2. Thomas Hout, Michael E. Porter, and Eileen Rudden, "How Global Companies Win Out," *Harvard Business Review*, September–October 1982.

3. Usually defined as carrying inventory, demand generation, physical distribution, after-sales service, and financing customer accounts.

customer selection, and so the distributor is judged against efficiency or cost-minimization criteria. Although some more-established firms manage this trade-off with considerable sophistication, all too often the delegation of marketing strategy to what is essentially a distribution organization results in underperformance, as nobody is in fact formulating a marketing strategy (this is discussed at length in Chapter 5).

In practice, these unique characteristics mean that marketing strategy in the international arena changes rapidly as the business grows or fails to grow. Importantly, it is driven not only by market characteristics (the basis for marketing strategy in the pure or theoretical sense), but also by organizational development, as the economics and knowledge of the local marketing unit develop. Indeed, it is usually impossible to separate the process of market development from the process of organizational development. It is possible, however, to identify commonalities across companies in this process of internationalization and so to describe the usual evolution of international marketing strategy. Such a framework has to begin by recognizing that different objectives for market entry may produce quite different outcomes in terms of entry mode and marketing strategy.

OBJECTIVES OF MARKET ENTRY

Companies enter international markets for varying reasons, and these different objectives at the time of entry should produce different strategies, performance goals, and even forms of market participation. Yet, companies frequently follow a standard market entry and development strategy. The most common, which will be described in the following section, is sometimes referred to as the "increasing commitment" pattern of market penetration, in which market entry is via an independent local distributor or partner with a later switch to a directly controlled subsidiary. This approach results from an objective of building a business in the country-market as quickly as possible but nevertheless with a degree of patience produced by the initial desire to minimize risk and by the need to learn about the country and market from a low base of knowledge. These might be described as straightforward financial objectives that are oriented around long-run profit maximization in the country, so this internationalization strategy could be described as the default option.

The fundamental reason for entering a new market has to be potential demand, of course, but nevertheless it is common to observe other factors driving investment and performance measurement decisions, such as:

LEARNING IN LEAD MARKETS

In some circumstances, a company might undertake a foreign market entry not for solely financial reasons, but to learn. For example, the white goods division of Koc, the Turkish conglomerate, entered Germany, regarded as the world's leading market for dishwashers, refrigerators, freezers, and washing machines both in terms of consumer sophistication and product specification. In doing so, it recognized that its unknown brand would struggle to gain much market share in this fiercely competitive market. However, Koc took the view that, as an aspiring global company, it would undoubtedly benefit from participating in the world's lead market and that its own product design and marketing would improve and enable it to perform better around the world.[4] In most sectors, participation in the "lead market" would be a prerequisite for qualifying as a global leader, even if profits in that lead market were low. The lead market will vary by sector: the United States for software, Japan for consumer electronics and telecommunications, France or Italy for fashion, and so on.

The important point about such an objective for market entry is that it will change the calculus of the market entry mode decision. If a company is to maximize learning from a lead market, for example, it will need to participate with its

---

4. Robin Root and John Quelch, "Koc Holding: Arcelik White Goods," Harvard Business School case study 9-598-033. Boston: Harvard Business School Publishing.

own subsidiary and a cadre of its own executives. Learning indirectly, via a local distributor or other partner, is obviously less effective and will contribute less to the company's development as a global player, even if short-term profitability is superior because of the lower investment required.

COMPETITIVE ATTACK OR DEFENSE

In some situations, market entry is prompted not by some attractive characteristics of the country identified in a market assessment exercise, but as a reaction to a competitor's move. The most common scenario is market entry as a follower move, when a company enters the market simply because a major competitor has done so. This is obviously driven by the belief that the competitor would gain a significant advantage if it were allowed to operate alone in that market, and so it is most common in concentrated or even duopolistic industries. Another frequent scenario is "offense as defense," in which a company enters the home market of a competitor—usually in retaliation for an earlier entry into its own domestic market. In this case, the objective is also to force the competitor to allocate increased resources to an intensified level of competition. In both cases, a company will have to adapt its strategies to the particular strategic stakes: rather than focusing on market development, the firm will set market share objectives and be prepared to accept lower levels of profitability and higher levels of marketing expenditure. This requires different performance standards and budgets from the usual scenario of low-risk entry and long-run development, and the company's control system must have sufficient flexibility to adapt to this. The overriding competitive objective should also be taken into account when considering whether and how to participate in the market with a local distributor or partner. Certainly, the low-intensity entry modes, such as import agents and trading houses, would be inappropriate unless the local partner will accept the lower profit expectations.

SCALE ECONOMIES OR MARKETING LEVERAGE

A number of objectives result from internationalization undertaken as what is sometimes described as a "replication strategy," in which a company seeks a larger market arena in which to exploit an advantage. In many manufacturing industries, for example, internationalization can help the company achieve greater economies of scale, particularly for companies from smaller domestic country-markets. In other cases, a company may seek to exploit a distinctive and differentiating asset (often protected as intellectual property), such as a brand, service model, or patented product. In both cases, the emphasis is on "more of the same," with relatively little adaptation to local markets, which would undermine scale economies or diminish the returns from replication of the winning model. To achieve either of these objectives, a company must retain some control, so it may enter markets with relatively high-intensity modes, such as joint ventures. In particular, either franchising or licensing are business models naturally suited for the rapid replication of businesses through expansion of units since both are centered on protected and predefined assets.

Apart from these varied marketing objectives, it is also common for governments to "incentivize" their country's companies to export, in which case the company may enter markets it would otherwise not have tackled. In summary, given the rapid business evolution that has been identified as one of the distinctive characteristics of international markets, it is reasonable to suppose that, for most companies, international operations will consist of a patchwork of country-market operations that are pursuing different objectives at any one time. This, in turn, would suggest that most companies would adopt different entry modes for different markets. More commonly, however, companies have a template that is followed in almost all markets. This usually starts with market entry via an indirect distribution channel, usually a local independent distributor or agent.

MODES OF MARKET ENTRY

The central managerial trade-off between the alternative modes of market entry is that between risk and control. On the one hand, low intensity modes of entry minimize risk. Thus, contracting with a local distributor requires no investment in the country-market in the form of offices, distribution facilities, sales personnel, or marketing campaigns. Under the normal arrangement, whereby the distributor takes title to the goods (i.e., buys them) as they leave the production facility of the international company, there is not even a credit risk, assuming that the distributor has offered a letter of credit from its bank. This arrangement also minimizes control, however, since the international company will have little or no involvement in most elements of the marketing plan, including how much to spend on marketing, distribution arrangements, and service standards. In particular, it should be noted here that effective control over marketing operations is impossible without timely and accurate market information, such as customer behavior, market shares, price levels, and so on. In many cases, low-intensity modes of market participation cut off the international firm from this information, since third-party distributors or agents jealously guard the identity and buying patterns of their customers for fear of disintermediation. Such control can only be obtained via higher-intensity modes of market participation, involving investments in local executives, distribution, and marketing programs. This is truly a trade-off in that companies cannot have it all, but must find compromise solutions. The fact is that control only comes from involvement, and involvement only comes from investment.

Another vital distinction here is between financial risk and marketing risk. It is financial risk that is usually the major consideration at the point of market entry, and it is financial risk that is minimized by low-intensity modes of market participation. However, this risk comes at the price of low control over business strategy, so that in fact marketing risk is maximized, with a local partner making all the important marketing decisions. It is the desire for greater control over the business (i.e., to minimize marketing risk) that explains the usual evolutionary pattern of increasing commitment.

The alternative modes of entry can therefore be distinguished by where each falls on the risk-control trade-off (see Figure 3–1). In addition, there are a number of points that should be borne in mind about each.

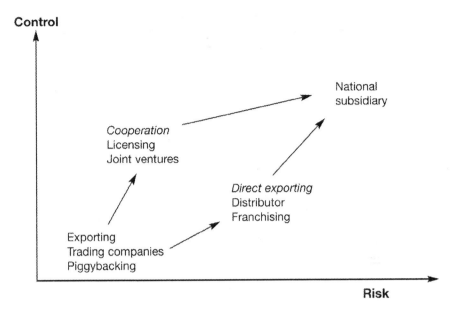

FIGURE 3–1 The Market Entry Mode Decision

EXPORT/IMPORT AND TRADING COMPANIES

Serving an international market through export/import agents, or trading companies such as the Japanese trading houses or the former British *hongs* in Hong Kong, is attractive in that it offers both low financial risk and access to substantial local operating knowledge. It is particularly suitable for companies with little international experience since almost all international operating functions are borne by the agent, including the costly and time-consuming requirements such as bills-of-lading, customs clearance, and invoice and collection. However, in addition to the low level of control, a couple of additional drawbacks should be noted. First, agents such as these operate on the basis of economies of scope, seeking to act as intermediaries for as many vendors as possible—they are servants of many masters. In many cases, therefore, the international vendor will be only a small proportion of the agent's business, so the vendor may end up feeling underserved by the agent, who, if acting rationally, will at any time devote the greatest attention to the vendor that offers the greatest total margin in a given period. Second, agents often operate on a commission basis, and they do not actually buy the goods from the international vendor, so there is a credit and cash flow risk that is not present in distributor arrangements.

"PIGGYBACKING"

Although such arrangements are rarely featured in international business texts, many companies begin their internationalization opportunistically through a variety of arrangements that may be described as "piggybacking," because they all involve taking advantage of a channel to an international market rather than selecting the country-market in a more conventional manner. For example, a firm may be offered some spare capacity on a ship or plane by a business partner, or it may find that a domestic distributor is already serving an international market and so grants a foreign distribution license that requires nothing more than an increase in domestic sales. An example of this is the Italian rice firm F&P Gruppo, owners of the leading Gallo brand, which entered Poland via their Argentinean subsidiary rather than direct from Italy, thus leading to the rather bizarre situation of packets of rice with Spanish-language packaging covered in stickers in Polish. The reason, it transpires, was that the Argentinean air force was importing freight from Poland via regular flights, but it was sending over empty aircraft on the outward leg, a source of export distribution capacity that was bought by a consortium of local food companies.[5]

The most common form of piggybacking is to internationalize by serving a customer who is more international than the vendor firm. Thus, a customer requests an order, delivery, or service in more than one country, and the supplier starts selling internationally in order to retain the customer and increases its penetration of the account. This is particularly

---

5. Nathalie Laidler and John Quelch, "Gallo Rice," Harvard Business School case study 9-593-018. Boston: Harvard Business School Publishing.

common in the case of business-to-business companies and technology-oriented start-ups. Another common situation is when two companies in the same industry combine to use the same distribution channel for products that are not directly competitive, thus obviating to some extent the financial disadvantage of establishing distribution when sales volumes are still low. Thus, for example, Minolta piggybacked on IBM's international distribution network, which helped Minolta achieve otherwise unaffordable distribution and helped IBM defray the cost of the distribution network. Similarly, competitors in some industries, such as pharmaceuticals, routinely license their sales and/or distribution to each other in markets where the competitor is better established and the products are not directly competitive.

When piggybacking via distributors or other comparable partners, the main disadvantage, in addition to the obvious lack of control, is the greater marketing risk that comes from not having studied the market potential and structure. The likely result is a short-term boost in sales, since this was the nature of the opportunity, but a medium-term problem arising from the unsuitability of the country-market, which was not analyzed before entry.

In the case of piggybacking via a major customer, the dangers are quite different. In fact, the level of control is likely to be quite high, given that internationalization has occurred in the context of a preexisting interorganizational relationship. However, in these cases, the supplier firm often underestimates the commitment required. To offer anything like the levels of service and customer relationship management to which the client is accustomed in the home market, it will almost certainly be necessary to establish an office, hire some local account managers, and establish a service operation for the customer's local operations. In addition, further expansion beyond the entry account may prove to be hampered by the fact that the products sold to that account were customized to the client in question and therefore not immediately transferable to the wider market.

FRANCHISING

Franchising is an underexplored entry mode in international markets, but it has been widely used as a rapid method of expansion within major developed markets in North America and Western Europe, most notably by fast food chains, consumer service businesses such as hotel or car rental, and business services. At heart, franchising is suitable for replication of a business model or format, such as a fast-food retail format and menu. Since the business format and, frequently, the operating models and guidelines are fixed, franchising is limited in its ability to adapt, a key consideration in employing this entry mode when entering new country-markets. There are two arguments to counter this. First, the major franchisers are increasingly demonstrating an ability to adapt their offering to suit local tastes. McDonald's, for example, is far from being a global seller of American-style burgers, but it offers considerably different menus in different countries and even different regions of countries.[6] In such cases, the format and perhaps the brand is internationally consistent, but certain customer-facing elements such as service personnel or individual menu choices can be tailored to local tastes. Secondly, it must be recognized that there are product-markets in which customer tastes are quite similar across countries. A business installing and maintaining swimming pools, for example, is a prime candidate for franchising, as sourcing and operations remain key success factors and are more or less universal. This is an example of a business, like fast food, that is not culture bound and in which marketing knowledge (i.e., the product- or service-specific knowledge involved in marketing this particular offering) is at least as important as local market knowledge (i.e., the knowledge required to operate successfully in a particular territory). It is also important to note that in such businesses, the local service personnel are a vital differentiating factor, and these will obviously still be local in orientation even if they operate within an internationally consistent business format.

---

6. One of McDonald's notably successful menu innovations has been in France, where it offers local regional specialties in its outlets in six to eight different regions of the country.

The main drawback of franchising is the difficulty of adapting the franchised asset or brand to local market tastes—even experienced corporations like McDonald's or Marriott, which have managed to thrive on this trade-off as discussed above, have taken several decades and some false starts to get to this point of advanced practice. A key indicator that franchising carries this constraint is the fact that marketing budgets at local levels are usually restricted to short-term promotions rather than market development. This is consistent with the concept that franchising is a rapid replication strategy. For example, consider the expansion of U.S.-based Weight Watchers into Mexico. Weight Watchers is a highly successful dieting business that franchises its programs to operators of local clubs and groups of people motivated to lose weight and maintain their new lighter shape. Its expansion into Mexico, which was the result of an opportunistic network initiative by a member of the U.S. executives' network, encountered some cultural differences compared with the United States or Canada. In some parts of the country, the attitude still prevailed that being overweight was not bad because it indicated sufficient affluence to eat well. In addition, Mexican consumers were far less nutritionally aware than their northern counterparts, who encountered extensive nutritional information on all food products by law. Clearly, market development required heavy local investment in market education to establish the dieting club concept. Because it was a franchise organization, however, the local marketing funds held by the entrepreneurial and small-scale group operators were much below what was necessary. While some franchising organizations allocate larger marketing budgets from central funds, it remains true that local marketing plays only a limited role in the replication strategy for which franchising is best suited.

LICENSING

Licensing is a common method of international market entry for companies with a distinctive and legally protected asset, which is a key differentiating element in their marketing offer. This might include a brand name, a technology or product design, or a manufacturing or service operating process.

Licensing is a practice not restricted to international markets. Disney, for example, will license its characters to manufacturers and marketers in categories such as toys and apparel even in its domestic market while it focuses its own efforts on its core competencies of media production and distribution. But it offers a particularly effective way of entering foreign markets because it can offer simultaneously both a low-intensity (and therefore low risk) mode of market participation and adaptation of product to local markets. Continuing with Disney as an example, its many licensing arrangements in China allow its characters to adorn apparel or toys suited to local taste in terms of color, styling, or materials.[7] This is because, as is usual in licensing agreements, the local licensee has considerable autonomy in designing the products into which it incorporates the licensed characters. The other major advantage of licensing is that, despite the low level of local involvement required of the international licensor, the business is essentially local and is in the shape of the local business that holds the license. As a result, import barriers such as regulation or tariffs do not apply.

As always, there are disadvantages, and two in particular should be factored into any decision on licensing. First, although it facilitates the creation of localized product, licensing is characterized by very low levels of marketing control. The licensee usually has to obtain approval from the international vendor for product design and specification, but it usually enjoys almost total autonomy over every other aspect of the marketing program (even if the contract includes constraints such as minimum price levels or promotional budgets). This is because the licensee is not a representative of the international vendor and, compared to a distributor or franchisee, is much more of an independent business that licenses only one specific and closely defined aspect of the marketing offer rather than acting as the *de facto* marketing

---

7. David J. Arnold, "Midway: Licensing, Distributing, and Building Brands in China," Harvard Business School case study 9-02-032. Boston: Harvard Business School Publishing.

arm of the international vendor. Second, and perhaps most importantly, licensing runs the risk of creating future local competitors. This is particularly true in technology businesses, in which a design or process is licensed to a local business, thus revealing "secrets," in the shape of intellectual property that would otherwise not be available to that local business. In the worst case scenario, the local licensee can end up breaking away from the international licensor and quite deliberately stealing or imitating the technology. This might arise from malicious intent or simply a breakdown in relations, as is not uncommon between an international company and its local partner (see Chapter 5). Even in a best case scenario, the local licensee will certainly benefit from accelerated learning related to the technology or product category—this is inevitable since the international company must by definition have a superior asset if there is a market for licensing it in the country. Over time, even absent of malicious intent, the local firm is likely to develop into a position in which it can launch its own rival business. Participation in international markets via licensing is therefore best suited to firms with a continuous stream of technological innovation because those corporations will be able to move on to new products or services that retain a competitive advantage over "imitator" ex-licensees.

These particular low-intensity modes of market participation are the most frequently adopted at the time of market entry, although franchising and licensing are less common than entry via an independent local distributor—perhaps because they involve rather more complex interorganizational contracts and managerial processes. In situations in which a replication strategy is adopted and rapid expansion of the business is a priority, they are highly suitable, and to that extent they are underutilized. In all cases, it is clear that the organizational arrangement and the marketing strategy are interrelated: the less involved the international company, the less likely it is to develop locally customized offers and the more likely it is to follow a replication strategy. In fact, a replication strategy can run counter to the overarching objectives in entering the market in the first place, as much recent experience in the large emerging markets demonstrates.

MARKETING ENTRY STRATEGIES— LEARNING FROM EMERGING MARKETS

Just as the internationalization boom of the 1990s proved instructive with regard to market assessment, so there is much to be learned from the marketing strategies adopted at entry by western companies in emerging markets.[8] While most attention has been paid to market entry mode questions, such as the choice between a joint venture or a subsidiary, it is notable that most multinationals made the same assumption about their marketing entry strategy—namely, that they would replicate the competitive strategy that had served them well in developed markets, transferring their developed market brands and strategies to emerging economies without adaptation. While an argument can be made for such a replication strategy on the grounds of leveraging competitive assets such as brand names, it can only be made by ignoring the fundamental tenet of marketing, which is that companies should responsively adapt their offerings in the face of different market conditions. The result in most cases has been an unprofitable niche position, in which MNCs compete with each other for the business of the small elite who value their brands and can afford their prices. That this position is the wrong one for multinationals is evidenced by their subsequent struggles, many aspects of which flow directly from this marketing approach. The surprisingly rapid growth

8. David J. Arnold and John Quelch, "New Strategies in Emerging Markets," *Sloan Management Review*, Vol. 40, No. 1 (Fall 1998). See also C. K. Prahald and Kenneth Lieberthal, "The End of Corporate Imperialism," *Harvard Business Review*, July–August 1998, and Niraj Dawar and Amitava Chattopadhyay, "Rethinking Marketing Programs for Emerging Markets," *Long Range Planning*, Vol. 35, No. 5 (October 2002): 457–474. This section also draws upon the benefits of joint research conducted with Professor Niraj Dawar of the University of Western Ontario.

of local brands, many of which imitate their global competitors, demonstrates that distribution, for example, is an achievable goal when it is part of an integrated market-driven approach. The fierce competition among multinationals is also indicative of "me-too" niche marketing strategies driven by replication rather than local market responsiveness, and it is evidence of a flawed execution of the original market entry strategy (to judge from the MNCs' declared objectives in entering emerging markets) of market penetration.

To turn around their business in these markets, multinationals must in effect reenter the markets by rethinking their marketing strategy at two levels. First, they must embrace a mass-marketing mindset. While most MNCs have lost the mass-marketing competence that made them huge corporations in the first place (because of the intensified competition and fragmentation that has developed in their home markets), this approach is suitable both for current conditions in emerging markets and for the market penetration objectives behind their market entries. This mindset, which includes the need for aggressive attention to price competitiveness, should be reintroduced as the medium-term goal of the MNCs in emerging markets. Secondly, MNCs must develop dynamic strategies for reaching those mass markets; in effect, market expansion strategies that will take them out of the elite niche.

There are two major reasons why multinationals should adopt a mass-marketing approach in emerging markets. First, it is demanded by the typical emerging market structure. Second, anything else is inconsistent with the rationale behind the entry of multinationals into these markets, which was market penetration that was justified by the high potential of large and/or economically undeveloped populations. The principal reason why these billions of people are described as potential consumers rather than categorized into market segments is that they lack the financial resources to purchase the multinationals' products. The affordability gap will only be bridged when companies reach down to them by offering products at affordable prices; it will not be realized by emerging market populations increasing wealth to the point at which they trade up to the products currently on offer.

In practice, however, most multinationals did not develop localized products as part of their entry strategy, instead preferring to transplant offerings from their traditional developed markets. Even disregarding the question of whether the product met local needs, this is a niche strategy because of the price position that such products inevitably occupy. Keen to maintain a degree of global price consistency and unable to lower the price much because of the threat of parallel importing, these transplanted products end up being priced at points at which only 3–5 percent of the population can afford them. It is this niche strategy that has given local competitors the space to develop their own competence and brands far more quickly than multinationals had anticipated. It also fitted well with the niche distribution strategy adopted by most multinationals, which tend to rely on larger channels with which they are somewhat familiar and which cannot realistically achieve high distribution coverage of the traditional, complex, socially embedded channels characteristic of emerging markets.

In short, multinationals were pursuing marketing strategies that were fundamentally inconsistent with their declared objective of entering emerging markets to realize the mass-market potentials of their huge populations. This is particularly ironic for that large number of multinationals that trace their own historical roots to the development of mass marketing in North America and Western Europe in the early and mid-twentieth century. While it might be argued that, given a long enough time frame, this potential will be realized, the only circumstances in which this justifies such early entry is when first-mover advantage can be obtained.

Mass marketing, as explained by business historian Richard Tedlow, began with the "breakthrough idea" of "profit through volume."[9] The alternative business paradigm, that of keeping prices and margins high, was dominant in the era preceding mass marketing and is increasingly a hallmark of the "era of segmentation," which characterizes most developed

---

9.   Richard S. Tedlow, *New and Improved: The Story of Mass Marketing in America* (Boston: Harvard Business School Press, 1999).

markets now. In these developed markets, marketing strategies begin with breaking down demand into well-defined segments and developing brands and products narrowly targeted
at those segments—almost the complete opposite of mass
marketing. By contrast, mass marketing was built around
good but simple products, narrow product ranges, and low
rates of product obsolescence.

Contrast these two marketing paradigms, and it is easy to
understand why the multinationals failed to adopt a mass-marketing approach—not only had they lost the required skills,
but they were actively attempting to move in the other direction, adapting their marketing approaches towards the "segment of one" era that technology promises in developed
markets. Speak to executives in these multinationals, however, and it becomes clear that the entry strategies that they
followed were by choice rather than forgetfulness. In many
cases, they argue, mass marketing is not yet possible in most
emerging markets because the marketing infrastructure on
which such strategies depend, especially distribution systems,
are not yet sufficiently developed. Casting the issue as a
"chicken-and-egg" problem in this way is a blinkered
approach for two reasons. First, Tedlow demonstrates that
mass marketing was not an inevitable product of technological
advances in manufacturing or distribution. Instead, it was
stimulated by the vision of a set of entrepreneurs (such as
Henry Ford) who sought to "democratize consumption" and
reap the first-mover benefits of building scale in operations
and customer franchise. This suggests that the multinationals'
niche marketing strategies represent a strategic failure rather
than a market failure. Second, there are companies managing
to penetrate the mass market.

The case of Kellogg, the U.S. cereals giant, demonstrates
that it is not only local competitors who can sense the need for
mass marketing and deliver it. Kellogg, lured by the prospect of
a billion breakfast eaters, ventured into India in the mid-1990s.
Like many of its counterparts, Kellogg's market entry strategy
proved unsuccessful, and, after three years in the market, sales
stood at an unimpressive $10 million. Indian consumers were
not sold on breakfast cereals. Most consumers either prepared

breakfast from scratch every morning or grabbed some biscuits with tea at a roadside tea stall. Advertising positions common in the west, such as the convenience of breakfast cereal, did not resonate with the mass market. Segments of the market that did find the convenience positioning appealing were unable to afford the international prices of Kellogg's brands. Disappointing results led the company to reexamine its approach. Eventually, Kellogg realigned its marketing to suit local market conditions: the company introduced a range of breakfast biscuits under the Chocos brand name. Priced at Rs. 5 (10 U.S. cents) for a 50-gram pack (and with extensive distribution coverage that includes roadside tea stalls), they are targeted at the mass market and are expected to generate large sales volumes. Other emerging market veterans such as Unilever, Colgate Palmolive, and South African Breweries have amply demonstrated the viability of mass markets in emerging economies and the benefits of rapidly transferring knowledge gained in one emerging market to others.

Another argument articulated by some multinationals is that emerging market consumers are rapidly becoming more like their affluent market counterparts, and that it is therefore sensible to offer globally standardized products and wait for the consumer to evolve towards a preference for these. This convergence argument may or may not be true, but it is certain that the rate of change is slow; specifically, in most emerging markets, the mass market will remain poor well beyond the current planning horizons of most multinationals. Even as they grow more affluent, it is far from certain that Chinese and Indian consumers' preferences will converge with those of Europeans or Americans. It is as likely that they may retain idiosyncratic local consumption patterns that are driven by cultural norms. A better strategy for any serious emerging market player is to understand and cater to local consumers' current needs and evolve with them as they grow more affluent.

There are two general approaches to moving towards mass-market strength that correspond to a fundamental choice that MNCs must make about the basis and nature of competition. On the one hand, MNCs must decide the basis on which they wish to compete in emerging markets. They can do so by either transferring their global assets, such as brand names of proven strength in other countries, or by developing local (i.e., market-specific) sources of advantage, which include but are not restricted to brand names. In addition, there is the related question of whether to compete against other MNCs or against local competition. These are, of course, interrelated questions, and the strategies are not mutually exclusive. Nevertheless, they represent quite different uses of marketing resources, and they will thus be manifested in distinctive marketing strategies.

The choices made by most MNCs until now are clear. For the most part, they have chosen to leverage their global assets, including brands, managers, and suppliers of marketing services, in the belief that these represented their sources of competitive advantage and that they would be valued in emerging market economies. In theory, this is a justifiable entry strategy if the MNC accepts the consequent restrictions on market size. In practice, this has led to overcompetition and rapid saturation of the wealthy segment of emerging market populations, principally because of the number of MNCs that entered these markets in a short period. In effect, this approach assumes that the advantages possessed by these companies are the output of previous marketing executives (e.g., established brands) rather than the ability of the current marketing executives to adapt the corporations' marketing assets and programs to new markets. This overconservative approach represents a failure to commit to the new emerging markets.

There are two principal routes of localization. The first is based upon the use of global sources of advantage, but it involves the MNC adapting its marketing mix to make that global asset more suited to local emerging market conditions. For example, an MNC might transfer an established global brand into an emerging market but change its packaging size, price points, or even its product formulation to enhance its attraction to the emerging market retailer and consumer. (Kellogg's approach in India is an example of this degree of localization.) It is important to note that this strategy does leverage the

MNC's global assets (i.e., it is not based upon marketing derived ground-up from analysis of the local market). However, it is more than simply exporting a global brand via a local distributor—the necessary adaptation requires investment. Importantly, this strategy also brings the MNC into competition with local players.

An alternative strategy is to develop new market-specific resources, a more direct but more costly and probably a slower approach than adaptation. This strategy is starting to be seen in the form of a number of MNCs acquiring local brands that are added to their portfolio alongside global counterparts. In Japan, for example, Coca-Cola carries a number of locally-oriented brands, such as Georgia iced coffee, that enable it simultaneously to meet local taste segments and to derive greater economies of scope from its sales and distribution investments in the country. Alternative local resources that might be developed are distribution assets, such as company-specific warehouses or fleets of vans or even bicycles. P&G took this approach in certain Eastern European markets. In these former communist states, the distribution systems were not simply undeveloped—they had completely collapsed. Recognizing that intensive distribution was an enabling condition for the development of their consumer goods business, P&G invested substantial sums in developing its own distribution network. It did so by funding distributor businesses in the form of vans, information technology, working capital, and extensive training.[10] This model, known within the company as the "McVan Model," produced a significant competitive advantage over both international and local competition; in Russia, for example, the development of 32 regional distributors, with 68 further subdistributors, resulted in P&G having distribution coverage of some 80 percent of the population at a time when most multinationals were still restricted to marketing in the two main cities of Moscow and St. Petersburg. This bold approach illustrates perfectly the trade-off between control and

10. David J. Arnold, "Procter & Gamble: Always Russia," Harvard Business School case study 9-599-050. Boston: Harvard Business School Publishing.

risk—considerable investment was required to develop this network in a country renowned as a distribution challenge (being the largest country in the world in terms of area), but by tackling the issue head-on rather than waiting for the enabling condition to develop, P&G gained huge leads in market share in many categories. While this advantage has continued in some countries, the financial commitment makes P&G far more vulnerable to economic shocks, such as the Russian financial crisis of the summer of 1998.

In summary, recent experiences in emerging markets strongly suggest that replication strategies, typically executed with low-risk forms of market participation, result in market skimming rather than true market penetration and development. This has been particularly ironic because market entry was undertaken ostensibly to develop high-volume businesses in these high-population countries. In practice, it seems likely that, over the long run, multinationals will follow the established template for internationalization by gradually increasing their involvement in the market and the extent to which they adapt their marketing programs to local consumer tastes.

A FRAMEWORK FOR THE EVOLUTION OF MARKETING STRATEGIES IN AN INTERNATIONAL MARKET

The process of business development in an individual foreign country-market consists of a sequence of distinct business challenges, and this evolution produces a sequence of marketing strategies and marketing organizations. This evolution, originally described in the conceptual paper by Susan P. Douglas and C. Samuel Craig from which Figure 3–2 is adapted,[11] consists of three principal phases: (1) a low-commitment

---

11. Susan P. Douglas and C. Samuel Craig, "Evolution of Global Marketing Strategy: Scale, Scope, and Synergy," *Columbia Journal of World Business* (Fall 1989).

	Initial Market Entry	Local Market Expansion	Global Rationalization
Key objective	Assessment and testing of new market opportunities	Achieve economies of scope to leverage local operating unit	Economies of scale to leverage presence
Managerial focus	Corporate center driving international expansion	Local management seeking local performance improvement	Regional and corporate managers seeking consolidation of multidomestic network
Marketing objective	Seek new geographical opportunities for existing marketing assets	Develop new market-specific marketing assets to maximize local market share	Identify marketing assets with global potential and seek consistent management
Marketing organization	Partnerships with independent local marketing firms	Delegation to local marketing management	Seek opportunities for knowledge and personnel transfer around network

FIGURE 3–2   The Evolution of International Marketing Strategy (*Source: adapted from Douglas and Craig*)

market entry, in which the MNC seeks incremental sales with minimum investment and is in effect testing the market; (2) a phase of intensified local marketing activity to develop business beyond the platform achieved in market entry and maximize performance within the country; (3) the consolidation of national units into a more integrated and efficient global marketing organization. Although some start-up firms appear to telescope this incremental internationalization into a "born global" or "big bang" expansion (see Chapter 7), it remains the dominant pattern. The evolution of the corporation through these phases appears to accelerate with international experience—from a more laissez-faire attitude in early years of international operation to a deliberate and forceful approach as the firm becomes more dependent upon, and committed to, its international business. This reflects the organizational learning that occurs systematically during internationalization and highlights the fact that the objectives an MNC sets itself for its business in any individual country-market can be a function not only of characteristics of the country, such as market potential, stability, and existing business infrastructure, but also of its own corporate international experience, level of commitment to international markets, and relevant management resources.

In many ways, the initial phase is more concerned with sales rather than marketing. Given the international firm's focus on risk minimization and its lack of local knowledge, the distributor will usually take the easiest option of selling the newly available products to its existing customer base. Indeed, the distributor will usually have been selected on the basis of this customer base. In this initial phase, there is little adaptation to the local market because the low sales levels cannot support the fixed costs of developing a local offer and because the international firm is still learning about the market. In fact, the only circumstance in which the international company is clearly targeting a segment of customers is when its broader international marketing strategy is based upon an international segment. In consumer markets, Nike, for example, addresses similar segments in multiple countries; in business to business markets, the customer is often international. Only when the distributor has exhausted the growth possibilities of "picking the low-hanging fruit" does the challenge of marketing arise with the need to target new customers or segments or introduce new product lines, in order to maintain growth.

It is often at this point that the international company takes over distribution and begins to invest in its own marketing organization in the country-market. Once this organization is in place, the range of products and services expands rapidly, often including new offers developed specifically for the local market. In this stage, the emphasis on local market development results in a marketing focus not unlike that in the domestic market or any other single market. Over time, however, the multinational firm can be expected to seek synergies across its global marketing network, both in terms of production and marketing economics, and market knowledge. It is also likely that it has a fully developed subsidiary in all developed markets, so it seeks consolidation to mirror the internationalization of its strategy. In the countries of the European Union, for example, many international firms are now shifting marketing strategy to a regional level, so they therefore realize that they do not need a senior marketing executive and team in each country.

There are a number of key learnings that experienced executives identify from this evolution:

GREATER COMMITMENT AT MARKET ENTRY

Increasingly, experienced companies seek closer control over marketing strategy at the time of market entry instead of delegating everything to a local distributor. This usually involves placing one or two appropriately qualified executives in-market alongside the local sales and distribution partner. The objective is to accelerate market development and maximize performance earlier in the process rather than relying on the distributor's customer base and then reaching a sales plateau (see Chapter 5).

LONG-TERM PLANNING AT MARKET ENTRY

Frequently, the appropriate market entry strategy is the wrong market development strategy. In other words, a company learns after a few years in the market that the distribution organization has the wrong coverage, it has been offering the wrong product lines, or some other aspect of the marketing offer is wrong. The probability of this is higher when the company has taken an opportunistic approach to market entry and has viewed the country as no more than a potential source of incremental sales of existing products that can be achieved with minimal risk or investment. The remedy is obviously to prepare a more rigorous plan for market development at the time of entry—one that is based upon the level of analysis of market potential and enabling conditions described in the previous chapter.

EARLY DEVELOPMENT OF LOCAL OR REGIONAL MARKETING PROGRAMS

Experienced multinationals are becoming far more capable of modular design in their products or services, identifying a core platform from which local variations can be more easily and economically developed. This enables earlier development of products tailored to local market conditions, which can be expected to accelerate market penetration. In many cases, the level at which products are customized is regional rather than country by country. This enables a multinational to retain some economies of scale while still adapting to local demand characteristics. Once a firm's international marketing network is well developed, such regional products may then be available at the time of market entry for other country-markets in the region.

These ways in which international firms are adapting the process of market development, based on accumulated experience, amount to a blurring of the three phases in the general framework described. Greater commitment at the time of market entry, for example, anticipates the increased investment and commitment previously seen at a later stage. Similarly, the development of regionally adapted products anticipates the integrated network and focus on international synergies characteristic of fully developed international marketing organizations.

Another important underlying dynamic, which experienced multinationals come to learn, is the distinction between market knowledge and marketing knowledge. Market knowledge is a local operating capability that is required for doing business in any country: it includes a knowledge of local regulatory requirements, business practices, negotiating styles, cultural norms, and a host of other details that add up to "the way people do business in a given country." Clearly, this cannot be acquired quickly by an outsider, so it explains why even the most experienced multinational will always need some sort of local partner at the time of market entry. Marketing knowledge, by contrast, is a global product-oriented capability: Anheuser Busch or Heineken know more about the marketing of beer than any local partner they take on because of years of experience in a wide range of markets and segments. Like local market knowledge, it cannot be acquired quickly by somebody new to the business. It is clear that both types of knowledge (market knowledge and marketing knowledge) are required to grow a business in a new international market. Inexperienced companies, however, tend to take on partners with extensive market knowledge and, because of their own stand-off approach and desire to minimize risk, assume that the local partner also has marketing knowledge. In fact, the companies that own a particular product or service are almost always the most knowledgeable marketers of it—this knowledge is behind the long-run desire of most companies to gain "control" of their international marketing operations in order to maximize sales and growth. To rely on a local partner's market knowledge to grow the business is to remove a vital engine of growth (in the form of well-developed marketing knowledge). This explains why experienced international companies are increasingly putting their own people alongside the local distributor or sales organization at the point of market entry.

SUMMARY

Even more than in start-up situations, evolutionary thinking is vital when entering and developing international markets. The central trade-off to be managed is between the requirements at entry and the different needs of the business once revenues and market coverage begin to grow. At the time of entry, the stance adopted by most international entrants is one of risk minimization, almost market testing, and this results in great reliance on a local partner. Over the longer run, however, most companies will want greater control and involvement. Different forms of entry mode provide different levels of control early on, but greater control is almost always associated with greater investment and commitment—and therefore greater exposure and risk. In addition, different forms of participation result in exposure to different types of risk: for example, licensing tends to be associated with competitive risk related to erosion of product and technology advantage; franchising increases the market risk of offering an unadapted product; and contracting with an independent distributor offers higher control over product but is associated with the risk of loss of control in other areas of the marketing mix.

The difficulties of adapting marketing strategy to the phase of product-market evolution are amply illustrated by the experience of many western multinationals in emerging markets since the wave of market liberalization began around 1990. Many have essentially replicated the strategies prevailing in their developed home markets, with careful targeting to the most immediately attractive segments. Given the interdependencies among markets resulting from the globalization of many companies, and in particular the threat of parallel importing, such replication can be seen as a prudent approach. It has not, however, facilitated market development at the rate projected by many companies at the time of market entry. In effect, these companies need to replicate the strategies they themselves adopted several decades earlier in opening up the mass markets in their own domestic economies— the original foundations of their current size and expertise.

The more sophisticated international marketing companies are now indeed finding ways of adapting to local market conditions, including new locally oriented brands, new distribution channels, and new thinking in areas such as pack size and pricing. The lesson from this wave of international market development is that marketing fundamentals, such as the importance of designing a marketing mix to meet local demand characteristics, remain a better guide to managerial decision making than the replication thinking that seems so logical in a globalized corporation.

4 GLOBAL BRANDING AND PROMOTION

The question of whether or not an international company should pursue a policy of global branding—whether it should seek globally consistent brand names, identities, and positions—encapsulates perfectly the core dilemma of international marketing. On the one hand, brands work because of their consistency and omnipresence, offering customers a short cut in the purchase decision by a promise of reliability and familiarity. It is also true, of course, that it is more efficient for companies to manage a single brand worldwide than a portfolio of different brands, both in terms of economies in marketing expenditure and in terms of managerial control and accountability. This suggests that brands should seek wide presence and a uniform identity on a global scale. On the other hand, it is also true that brands work because of the resonance of meaning and identity they offer to customers at a deep, sometimes emotional or subconscious, level. Indeed, many trends in the wider field of marketing are enabling marketing companies to get ever closer to their customers and even in some cases to customize their offering or messages to individuals. Until people are the same around the globe, therefore, we might expect brands to succeed when they reflect local and even individual taste and culture.

The debate on global branding is not a new one, and it has been conducted with almost evangelical fervor and little data.

Advocates of globalization have pointed to the convergence of culture and consumer taste around the world as the main justification for global branding. The seminal statement of this argument was made by Harvard Business School's Theodore Levitt in his influential 1983 paper "The Globalization of Markets":

> A powerful new force now drives the world towards a single converging commonality, and that force is technology.... The result is a new commercial reality—the emergence of global markets for standardized consumer products on a previously unimagined scale of magnitude. Corporations geared to this new reality benefit from enormous economies of scale in production, distribution, marketing, and management. By translating these benefits into reduced world prices, they can decimate competitors that still live in the disabling grip of old assumptions about how the world works. Gone are accustomed differences in national or regional preference.... Ancient differences in national tastes or modes of doing business disappear. The commonality of preferences leads inescapably to the standardization of products, manufacturing, and the institutions of trade and commerce.[1]

Not surprisingly, such strongly expressed views provoked opposition, fuelling the polemic with which we still live. The most influential "localization" paper was Susan P. Douglas and Yoram Wind's "The Myth of Globalization":

> The adoption of a strategy of universal standardization appears naïve and over simplistic ... such an approach as a universal strategy in relation to all markets may not be desirable, and may lead to major strategic blunders. Furthermore, it implies a product orientation, and a product-driven strategy, rather than a strategy grounded in a systematic analysis of customer behavior and response patterns and market characteristics.... The design of an effective global marketing strategy does not necessarily entail the marketing of standardized products and global brands worldwide.[2]

---

1. Theodore Levitt, "The Globalization of Markets," *Harvard Business Review* (May–June 1983).
2. Susan P. Douglas and Yoram Wind, "The Myth of Globalization," *Columbia Journal of World Business* (Winter 1987): 19–28.

To the antiglobalization lobby, the perceived unfolding of Levitt's doomsday scenario is a prime motivation for opposition to the spread of brands across the globe. To brand marketing executives within multinational companies, however, it is the resilience of local variations in taste that dominates their decision making, representing an ongoing challenge to any attempt to reap global economies of scale and control in marketing. Indeed, many multinationals, in consumer markets in particular, are adding local brands to their portfolio as eagerly as they are investing in global "power brands." Nevertheless, there is a sea of change occurring in this field two or more decades after Levitt made his bold predictions, although it is not driven by the convergence of consumer taste he forecast. Instead, internationalization at the intermediate level in the market system, specifically in retail distribution and in media, is enabling international companies to reap real and rapidly increasing benefits from pursuing global branding strategies. However, this only exacerbates the underlying dilemma—if consumer tastes remain variable around the world, does a global branding policy risk alienating the company's brands from its customer base?

This is the core dilemma of international marketing—companies are growing more global in their presence and their degree of integration, but consumers retain varying levels of local orientation in their tastes and demands. The challenge is therefore for companies to "think globally" by organizing their marketing in a way that enables them to benefit from globalization of the marketing industry but to retain the ability to "act locally" by communicating directly to local consumer taste where appropriate. This chapter explores how this can be achieved in the following way:

- The benefits and drawbacks of a global branding policy are examined at two different levels of the marketing system: international company and consumer.

- Brand policy is decomposed into issues of brand name, brand identity, brand positioning, and product.

- The benefits and costs of branding at these different levels are analyzed. It is recommended that global branding be restricted to the name and visual appearance.

■ Guidelines are suggested for a "buy globally, sell locally" approach, in which global economies of scale in marketing are achieved while retaining enough local flexibility for brand meaning to be related to local taste and culture.

This chapter does not address the argument of the antiglobalization lobby that global brands are threatening local culture and therefore producing global cultural impoverishment. Rather, the consistency with which consumers in any country reflect their values in brand choice, and therefore the power of brands to shape consumer decision making, is assumed, and attention is focused on the corporate dilemma of whether to seek global consistency of branding or to build a portfolio of local brands.

GLOBAL BRANDING TRENDS

It is, of course, true that a number of leading brands appear more frequently around the world. It is also true that global stature is increasingly a prerequisite for participation in the world's major promotional opportunities, such as the soccer World Cup, the biggest media event of all. Only a truly global brand will have the scale to afford the sponsorship of such a huge event and the consistency of identity to benefit from the global exposure provided by such an event, which is seen in almost every country of the world at the same time. It is also impossible not to acknowledge that developments in communications technology and media have made most of the world much more aware of events and tastes of other countries—Michael Jordan or Pelé are known around the world, as are Gucci shoes or Honda cars.

However, this is not necessarily indicative of a trend towards what a consumer would perceive as global branding—namely, fewer, more dominant brands in the world. In fact, the internationalization of these brands has usually stimulated the launch and/or growth of local brands in the same category, so that, while they enjoy increasing sales in an increasing market, their share of that market may not have increased as they have entered more and more countries.[3] The entry of McDonald's into the Philippines, for example, eventually provoked the establishment and growth of the local fast-food chain Jollibee, offering a menu of local dishes, such as spicy or sweet and sour burgers. Not only has Jollibee achieved success in its domestic market, but it has also entered McDonald's domestic U.S. market, and it is enjoying considerable success in California as an exotic alternative to the established fast-food chains.

From a corporate perspective, the picture is equally unclear. While the opportunities afforded by global branding are clear in terms of marketing expenditure and operations, companies are constrained by their administrative heritage and their global market positions. There are two major groups of companies. First are those that have grown to be global through what is described later in this chapter as an "export strategy." This applies to a company like Coca-Cola, which has entered international markets in a sequence of controlled moves, in the course of which the basic marketing mix elements of product and brand name have remained unchanged. The branding policies of such companies have always placed considerable emphasis on global consistency and retention of the brand's root identity. More recently, however, they have been seeking to add to this a level of local adaptation and identity, so as not to be seen as a monolithic and unresponsive global exporter. Examples include Coca-Cola's Georgia iced coffee, and Unilever's Ala cold-water laundry detergent, neither of which are available in the corporations' core western markets. This shift in emphasis is driven by a number of factors, including the maturation of consumer tastes, the improvement in the perceived quality of local brands (especially in emerging markets), and the antiglobalization lobby. The bellwether for such companies is

---

3. See the discussion of industry concentration and product proliferation in Chapter 1.

Coca-Cola, which since the appointment of Douglas Daft as the new CEO in 2000 has pronounced itself to be seeking a "return to our multidomestic roots."[4] It must be emphasized, however, that while such companies seek to adjust the identity of their brands in terms of user imagery or cultural tone, they continue to seek and enjoy the benefits of being global in terms of expenditure and marketing operations.

A quite different situation faces companies that have internationalized in a less organic way, particularly those that have entered markets by acquisition, such as the European giants Nestlé or Unilever. As a result of this history, such companies typically have a portfolio of local brands, each with a distinct national identity, heritage, and customer equity. For them, the challenge is to reorganize their operations so that they can begin to reap international economies in marketing. In many cases, this means a rationalization of the brand portfolio that includes at least some move towards global consistency.

Both trends are clearly visible in the current business environment. The end result is likely to be what can already be seen emerging in the leading consumer brand marketing companies—a portfolio that includes both a small number of "global power brands" and, in each country, a number of national or regional brands that address the distinct local variations in taste and demand. Given that almost all businesses start local and only later internationalize, it is the moves towards globalization of the brand portfolio that are the most common and salient. In particular, recent moves by brand giants Procter & Gamble and Unilever towards consolidation of their brand portfolios have been widely interpreted as the triumph of global branding: Unilever has publicly announced its goal of trimming its brand portfolio from 1,600 to 400 in five years, while Procter & Gamble has reorganized so that global brand management groups override the traditional country-based organizations. It should be emphasized, however, that these moves are driven more by distribution and media considerations than by a perceived convergence of consumer taste. In other

---

4. Douglas Daft, "Back to Classic Coke," *Financial Times*, March 27, 2000, p. 15.

words, Levitt's predictions of global power brands may be coming true, but not for the reasons he articulated.

This distinction between the corporate and consumer perspective is crucial. In fact, businesses benefit considerably more than consumers from global branding policies (with a few exceptions—most notably when businesses are the customers). It is therefore important to understand the different benefits and costs to each side of the exchange as a first step in designing an international branding policy.

BENEFITS OF GLOBAL BRANDS TO COMPANIES

The considerable benefits of global branding to marketing companies fall into three broad categories:

CONVERGENCE IN MARKETING SYSTEMS

While the degree of convergence of taste at the consumer level remains a topic of debate, there can be no doubt that at the intermediate levels of most market systems, such as distributors, retailers, and media, there has been considerable convergence, which continues apace. The most dramatic shift has been in media. The rapid growth of large media groups that followed the deregulation of broadcasting in many countries and the growth of the Internet have resulted in a profusion of media that crosses borders. Particularly in regions such as Europe, with a large number of relatively small neighboring countries, the former correlation of media with countries has disappeared, and both programming content and advertising are international. It is clearly more difficult for a company to make use of these media if brands are differently named in different countries: although such channels can offer national deals for advertisers and can broadcast different advertisements in different countries, this runs contrary to the company's international operating model, and it is a complex and therefore expensive task. This is particularly pertinent with regard to the fastest-growing area of promotion, namely event-related sponsorship. The growth of international media has played an important part in making major events, especially sports events, the most powerful promotional platforms available internationally. Only a global company with global brands can sponsor a tennis player or race-car driver who appears all over the world each year or place a field-side banner at a World Cup match with a global audience.

Retailers and other distributors have been slow to internationalize compared with their suppliers and customers, but they are now catching up fast. The growth of international retailers, for example, has already resulted in several major suppliers deciding to serve them internationally (either regionally or globally), and the growth of global account management, discussed more fully in Chapter 6, continues. It is clear that the ability to serve customers internationally will soon be a prerequisite for many vendors. This will certainly increase the benefits of global branding because only consistent brands will yield the purchasing economies of scale that many distributors are seeking. A retailer introducing pan-European purchasing, for example, will favor a regional brand over a portfolio of brands that have to be ordered, delivered, and managed separately for each country.

MARKETING ECONOMIES OF SCALE

While convergence of marketing systems requires consistency in positioning, there are also economic opportunities to be exploited from global brands. These fall into two categories. First, it is possible to leverage marketing resources across countries and so achieve economies of scale. Such resources might include packaging or certain sales material or promotions. If a marketing campaign or promotion that has been successful in one country is transferred to other country-markets, this can frequently prove cheaper than designing marketing platforms from scratch country by country. An advertising campaign, for example, might cost $1 million to produce; although this is minor relative to the media costs of broadcasting the advertising, a significant savings can nevertheless be made if the same campaign can be used in, say, 20 or more countries. Increasingly, suppliers such as agencies are internationally organized to facilitate such leverage.

Second, marketing economies of scale can be achieved by designing campaigns to be international from the outset and by executing international purchases of resources to execute such a design (for example, media time, promotional events, or collateral materials). An example of this would be the ability to launch a brand in many countries simultaneously rather than in the phased sequence of country launches. Not only does this give the launch greater momentum from the international critical mass, but it also squeezes the opportunity for response by competitors, which face immediate competition across all fronts. Similarly, brand extensions can be launched into either new categories or new country-markets much more efficiently and with a much greater chance of success when there is an established platform of brand awareness in other countries. These economies of scale in marketing (which are different from production-related scale economies in manufacturing) are the key to the vision of "global power brands" being pursued by a few of the major brand consumer giants. Their goal, which is already being realized in some situations, is to be able to outspend significantly competitor brands (at both trade and consumer level) through concentration of expenditure on a few brands that can benefit from international economies of scale in their marketing.

ORGANIZATIONAL BENEFITS OF GLOBAL BRAND MANAGEMENT

Finally, global branding represents a significant reduction in managerial complexity for the marketing company, and it thus offers organizational benefits. These may accrue in quantitative forms, such as a lower number of executives required in brand management or a simpler, more efficient decision-making processes. In addition, the framework of a common brand strategy will facilitate the transfer and leverage of marketing ideas from any one unit into the wider organization, and it will therefore reinforce the global consistency of brand management. Against this should be weighed the issue of local managerial resistance to global or corporate initiatives: a feeling of "ownership" of the business, customers, or marketing programs can often produce local resistance that is essentially territorial rather than being based upon a substantive market-based argument. For most multinationals, however, this represents a challenge to be overcome rather than a fundamental barrier to internationalization.

SUMMARY—THE BUSINESS OF MARKETING IS GLOBALIZING

There can be little doubt that the infrastructure of marketing, especially consumer marketing, is globalizing at a rapid rate. The internationalization of media, distributors, and marketing services firms offers significant benefits to those firms international enough in their marketing organization to deal on a global basis. These benefits may be financial (in the form of scale economies) or managerial (in the form of greater bargaining power or access to opportunities denied smaller local marketing organizations). International brand companies have little choice but to internationalize their organizations to deal with this new era of global marketing systems—any company that remains wholly local in its marketing management will soon find itself at a disadvantage, with greatly reduced power in dealing with intermediaries of all sorts.

There will remain local opportunities. Retail buyers, for example, have traditionally relied for much of their success on deals oriented around local variations in demand or production or their ability to offer or run in-store promotions in their own retail space. Indeed, the introduction of regional buying has been resisted even within some multinational retailers by managers whose incentives are embedded in relationships with local sales personnel and in the distinctive flow of production in local factories and promotions in local stores. Similarly, local markets for media remain vital given the variation in programming, news and events in different countries, and the national variation in ownership and regulation of media.

Nevertheless, there is little to be gained from not participating in the new globalized marketing industry, but there is much to be lost. Media and retail businesses stand to make clear gains from building globally integrated organizations, so they will therefore not reverse their moves towards this end state. As a result, brand marketing companies with any international ambition have to follow and build globalized marketing organizations.

BENEFITS OF GLOBAL BRANDS TO CONSUMERS

From the consumer perspective, the benefits of globally standardized brands are far less clear. Although most consumers are now offered a far more internationally varied range of brands and products in almost all categories, there is less evidence of convergence of taste. Indeed, the most notable single trend in the field of marketing in the first years of the new century is the new ability of companies to break down mass production and communication models and approach the ideal state of "markets of one," in which consumers are addressed and supplied as individuals. Despite this, the acceptance of many large brands in countries all around the world indicates that these global brands have wide appeal. It is therefore important to understand the nature of that appeal and to identify those contingencies that make global branding more likely to succeed.

WHEN FOREIGN ORIGIN IS EQUATED WITH SUPERIOR QUALITY

The most clearly recognized benefit of global brands—and the factor that explains much of the global spread of the world's most valuable brands—is their perceived superiority. In such circumstances, preference for international brands is a rational move on the part of the customer, as predicted by Levitt. It is important to note that quality should be viewed as widely as possible, encompassing not only superior functional attributes but also quality of experience, including novelty. In many emerging markets, for example, international food or drink brands are so different from traditional local products that comparison is difficult, but it is clear that the novelty of new categories explains much of the initial appeal of the new entrants. This aspect of the power of global brands has a number of interesting managerial implications:

- It explains the country of origin effect. So, for example, as long as German engineering is highly regarded, it will benefit German brand owners to emphasize their origin. This obviously assumes that consumers identify the country of origin, which in some cases can be falsified by use of a linguistic finesse (for example, the Argentinean food retailer Disco uses Bell's for its private label).
- It suggests that in emerging markets, where manufacturing and services are sometimes less developed than in the "triad" markets, international brands should emphasize their foreign origins and that they may be able to succeed with fewer adaptations to local taste at either the product or the branding level.
- It suggests that in business-to-business markets, in which product choice is often preceded by exhaustive and rational comparison of the alternative products available, a product that has a track record of success should be promoted as such, including any branding that is associated with the product.

The complication here is that product quality standards in any market are evolutionary, usually improving in line with economic growth. In other words, the perceived superiority of an international brand will last only as long as local brands are perceived to be inferior and will erode if the standards of local brands improve. In fact, there is plentiful evidence from emerging markets that the improvement of local brands, when stimulated by the entry of international brands into the market, is a fairly universal pattern. This pattern can be described by the graph shown as Figure 4–1—the international brands enjoy a honeymoon period of novelty and appeal, but over time the improvement of the local brands reduces their perceived superiority and thus their perceived value. This also explains the second point above. For example, an American

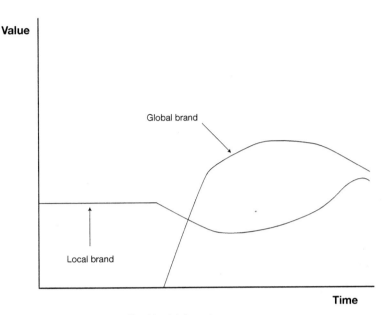

FIGURE 4–1 Evolution of Consumer Value Offered by Global Brands

food brand has a higher chance of achieving perceived product quality in an emerging market such as Poland than it does in Poland's more economically developed neighbor Germany. Interestingly, there are already signs that the improving quality of local products in the major emerging markets such as India and China is giving new challenges to the global brands that enjoyed such esteem there after their entry in the early 1990s: "China is emerging as an industrial power in its own right, [and] the best of China's consumer goods firms are also starting to outgrow this supporting-actor role.... Their growth in China over the past few years has been extraordinary."[5]

WHEN CUSTOMERS ARE INTERNATIONAL

For a global brand to offer distinctive benefits over and above local brands, it is not enough that customers be internationally dispersed. They must buy and experience the brand in an

---

5. "Chinese Brands: Out of the Shadows," *The Economist*, August 28, 1999.

internationally connected manner. In practice, most consumer markets fail this test—although an increasing number of consumers travel internationally and so occasionally purchase a brand in another country-market, these "purchases on the road" constitute only a trivial proportion of most markets and, given their out-of-the-ordinary nature, have little influence on underlying brand perceptions and preferences. In business-to-business markets, however, it is increasingly true that customers buy and use products internationally. Not only do many buying departments coordinate purchases internationally in order to achieve greater bargaining power and consistency in the products they purchase, but these products are often integrated across the international units of the organization. If a firm is using the same computers or telephones in different countries in order to support its internal network, it makes little sense for these products to be branded differently in different countries. It is also true that within a business, it is quite common for executives from one country to visit another and have their perceptions shaped by international experience far more than in almost all consumer markets.

WHEN BRANDS ARE ASPIRATIONAL AND CONSPICUOUSLY USED

Although a consumer generally selects a brand on the basis of individual and situation-specific needs and wants, there are occasions when the wider reputation of a brand is important. This wider reputation applies to brands that are conspicuously used by the consumer, such as cars or clothes, and contributes to the social image of the consumer who has chosen them. Because the brands have a social status function, consumers generally select the highest status brand they can afford in order to boost their image, making the brands "aspirational." In such cases, an image of global leadership can *per se* be of value to a consumer. The global brand badge can be interpreted as a sign that it is the world's best product and that the consumer is sophisticated and cosmopolitan enough to have selected it on this basis. Interestingly, it is in the premium sector of many product categories that one finds the most globally consistent brands. While this applies most obviously to fashion brands such as Gucci or status brands such as Rolex, it also applies to role models, such as sports or film stars, with whom people identify because they are perceived as leaders in their field. This probably explains the fact that the youth or teen segment is often identified as the most globally homogenous segment in many markets: if it is accepted that teens are particularly likely to identify with and be influenced by external role models, the internationalization of media is likely to have resulted in more standardized global role models.

SUMMARY—GLOBAL BRANDS HAVE A SPECIFIC BUT LIMITED APPEAL TO CONSUMERS

With the exception of these situations, there is no reason for a consumer to choose a brand because it is globally consistent. In fact, this would be a curious purchase criterion because global consistency can have little relevance to the consumer's needs and wants that are being satisfied by the brand. Rather, a consumer can be assumed to be making a self-centered brand choice based upon individual needs and wants: if he or she chooses a global brand, it is more likely to be because it satisfies those needs and wants rather than because it is globally available. Indeed, there is some limited evidence of a shift in consumer perception away from global brands towards brands with a local identity and heritage. Researchers into consumer culture, such as Harvard's Douglas Holt, are starting to document a "postmodern counterculture" that refuses to accept the authority of the market and gravitates towards "citizen" brands with a local heritage and identity.[6]

In summary, global branding strategies are likely to benefit companies far more than consumers, on average. There is a range of specific situations in which global brands may appeal to customers, but some of these are temporary, such as the period in which globalism confers an image of superior quality. Since a company should certainly seek to globalize its

---

6. Douglas B. Holt, "Why Do Brands Cause Trouble? A Dialectical Theory of Consumer Culture and Branding," *Journal of Consumer Research*, Vol. 29, No. 1 (June 2002).

marketing organization in order to reap the benefits of global operations but should also remain closely attuned to its market, the challenge is to "manage globally, sell locally." The key to managing this challenge is to understand the different levels of branding and to manage each differently.

WHAT IS A GLOBAL BRAND?

This deceptively simple question, when considered carefully, leads to the critical issue of whether brand identities are or should be managed consistently on an international basis. On one level, it is evidently true that there are a number of brands that are increasing in value, which derive an increasing proportion of their revenues from international markets and which enjoy an increasingly global presence and recognition. Research organizations regularly publish league tables of the world's most valuable brands (see Table 4–1), including both corporate and product brands, and when doing so, the foundation of their analysis is the global sales breakdown for products under the brand name in question.[7] At this level, the fact that the brand is sold globally is usually taken as an indication that it is a global brand; its owners see the increasing internationalization of its revenue base, and consumers, especially mobile consumers such as investors and business commentators, see the brand available in a greater range of locations.

Brands are more than just products or names. When discussed in a single-market context, it is always acknowledged that a brand is a sum of meanings and identities that reside at a deep level in the minds of its consumers. It is at this deeper level of meaning that the strength of a major brand is found— not just at the level of recognition and awareness. If a brand is

---

7. Note that this research approach favors corporate brands (i.e., those companies that apply their corporate name to all products) over product-level brands.

TABLE 4–1 "The Global Brand Scorecard"—Leading Brands by Value *(Source: "The Best Global Brands," BusinessWeek, August 5, 2002, pp. 95–96)*

RANK	BRAND	BRAND VALUE 2000 ($ BILLIONS)
1	Coca-Cola	69.64
2	Microsoft	64.09
3	IBM	51.19
4	GE	41.31
5	Intel	30.86
6	Nokia	29.97
7	Disney	29.26
8	McDonald's	26.38
9	Marlboro	24.15
10	Mercedes	21.01
11	Ford	20.40
12	Toyota	19.45
13	Citibank	18.07
14	Hewlett-Packard	16.78
15	American Express	16.29
16	Cisco	16.22
17	AT&T	16.06
18	Honda	15.06
19	Gillette	14.96
20	BMW	14.43
21	Sony	13.90
22	Nescafé	12.84
23	Oracle	11.51
24	Budweiser	11.35
25	Merrill Lynch	11.23

to be described accurately as a global brand, therefore, it must display some sort of global consistency in its positioning (or, in consumer terms, its identity). When examined in this light, it is clear that the brands in Table 4–1 represent different ways of achieving their global stature.

GLOBAL BRAND NAME AND VISUAL IDENTITY BUT LOCALLY ADAPTED PRODUCT AND/OR POSITIONING

At one extreme are products that are distributed globally but that display considerable local variation in terms of brand meaning and identity. McDonald's, for example, increasingly offers local menu items to complement the hamburger-and-fries staple on which the brand was built; in India it offers McTikka and the Big Maharajah, in France its menu includes wine, and in Germany beer. This recognition of differences in taste among cultures increases its local identity at the expense of its global image of an American fast-food chain. In some markets, especially emerging economies such as China, the company has also learned that it is not always viewed as a fast-food brand: in many of these countries, it is seen as a destination restaurant, in which a high proportion of customers seek to eat their meal at a leisurely pace on the premises. It is of course true that the visual identity of the brand remains globally consistent with the red-and-yellow of the "golden arches" (although local script such as Arabic or Chinese is used for the name of the outlet). But it is impossible for consumers to view McDonald's as a uniform American offer when local specialties are featured in the restaurants.

COUNTRY OF ORIGIN OR "EXPORT" BRANDS

The most sizeable group of brands in the global league tables is what might be described as the "country-of-origin" brands. An established stream of research into cross-cultural consumer behavior has validated the concept that consumers frequently attribute to brands the characteristics they associate with the brand's country of origin. Thus, German brands are seen as well-engineered and reliable, Italian brands as exciting and stylish, American brands as youthful and hedonistic, Japanese brands as innovative and technological, and so on. These national stereotypes are themselves a form of brand image, of course, and the country-of-origin effect testifies to the fact that they are often stronger brand images than those attached to the product itself. Companies occasionally acknowledge the strength of this effect through their choice of brand names. They might, for example, choose a French name for a fashion product or a Japanese name for an electronic product even when neither the company nor the factory is in that country. The largest group is American: Coca-Cola, Marlboro, Disney, Levi's, and others epitomize values of youthfulness, freedom, and individuality associated with the United States. For the most part, the brands from countries such as Japan, Germany, France, Britain, and others also draw upon associations of national stereotypes from their country of origin.

For many of these brands, their focused national image reflects their history. Coca-Cola, for example, followed American troops around the world in war years. This incremental internationalization, based on a homogenous target group, enabled the brand to retain what is essentially its domestic identity while broadening its international distribution. This can therefore accurately be described as an export strategy, focusing on distribution to new markets without adapting any other elements of the marketing mix. Such brands are therefore inherently global in character. What they share is a focus on their roots. These roots need not be geographical, but they could also be related to the brand's founder or designer, and so the category of export brands includes designer brands such as Christian Dior or Calvin Klein. It is ironic that the globalness of these brands (i.e., the fact they are positioned consistently) derives from a distinctly local image allied to an export strategy. It certainly makes international management of the brand a much simpler challenge than that facing companies that have internationalized through acquisition and as a result have a portfolio of local brands.

GLOBAL BRAND WITH VARIABLE PRODUCT—OR VICE VERSA

Finally, it is important to note the distinction between product and brand. In markets characterized by significant local variations in consumer taste, it is common for the same brand to be used for products that have been adapted to those local tastes. Some international brands of laundry detergent, for example, will be found with different fragrances in neighboring countries or with blue flecks in one country but green flecks in another. This reflects proven preferences of most consumers in those markets. Similarly, Coca-Cola, although a global brand in terms of name, appearance, and positioning, varies in terms of sweetness, color, and other functional respects to suit local tastes. Contrast these "same name adapted product" brands with their counterparts, the "same product different name" brands. Examples include the product known as Milky Way in North America but the Mars bar in Europe or the Ford car known as the Mondeo in Europe but the Contour in North America. Which of these is closest to a global brand strategy? It is clear that these are two separate issues. Product standardization is justified by economies of scale in operations; this can be translated into marketing (i.e., consumer-oriented) benefits if the lower production costs can be passed through as lower prices at the consumer level, thus improving the value proposition. But this decision will be made on the basis of the product-specific production considerations, such as whether manufacture can be consolidated into a few plants serving all the world or whether the bulk-to-value ratio demands a dispersed network of local production facilities. By contrast, the globalization of a brand name, while yielding some marketing economies of scale, is essentially a customer-driven decision. To the extent that customers will accept a globally standardized name, the marketing managers of a company can adopt a global branding strategy. It is likely that in almost all markets, some product variation may be necessary, not only because of differences in consumer taste and demand, but also because of local specifications in areas such as electricity, safety, measurement standards and systems, or even climate or servicing considerations. Given that production will be dispersed at least regionally in almost all product categories, there is usually little reason not to embrace local product adaptation. It is the branding decision that offers the greatest scope for globalization, and only brands with a global identity can be described as global brands, regardless of product variation.

The key distinctions, then, are among product, brand name, and brand positioning. (Brand name also usually implies an identical visual identity, such as logo and/or color choice.) International policy on product and brand names can be treated as two independent decisions because the possibilities are for all practical purposes unconstrained by interdependencies. The tension between brand name and brand positioning, by contrast, is both real and important. An understanding of this relationship is the foundation on which global branding policy should be built.

GUIDELINES FOR A GLOBAL BRANDING POLICY

Given the trends that have been identified, the challenge that a global branding policy must meet is to offer the company the opportunity to reap international economies of scale in marketing while simultaneously providing enough flexibility to adapt the brand to any local variations in customer perception or taste. The following section outlines a number of managerial guidelines for achieving this balancing act of global efficiency and local sensitivity.

GLOBALIZE AT THE LEVEL OF NAME AND APPEARANCE, BUT NOT BRAND MEANING

As a first step, it is important to decompose the brand into its constituent levels. As shown in Figure 4–2, a brand can be understood in terms of progressively deeper and more intimate levels of relationship with the consumer. The relationship begins with the relatively superficial brand name (which on its own is merely a label of recognition), includes the more complex level of brand identity and meaning (or, in managerial terms, its positioning), and ends with the actual experience

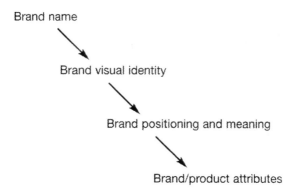

FIGURE 4–2   Levels of Branding

and satisfaction in use (which includes the product attributes). This mirrors the process by which a consumer relates to a brand: initially, the brand is recognized, stored perceptions of the brand are then invoked, and in the event of a purchase, the behavioral experience of the brand either reinforces or alters those stored perceptions. As has been observed, the product can vary among countries without influencing the higher levels of identity and recognition.

The critical question is the level at which international consistency is sought. In general, more experienced global brand marketing companies are retreating slightly from their earlier goals of building global brand personalities and meanings through the detail of their positioning. Whereas many companies entered the 1990s attempting to standardize brand name and positioning as far as possible (on the assumption of converging consumer taste and in order to achieve marketing economies of scale), many now accept that something as complex as the meaning of a brand to consumers can only converge as far as the point at which it meets local culture. Coca-Cola's Chairman and CEO Douglas Daft made the most articulate expression of this altered position and the reasons for it:

> We were heading in a direction that had served us very well
> for several decades, generally moving towards consolidation

and centralized control.... The world ... began moving in the 1990s in a different direction.... As globalisation accelerated, many national and local leaders understandably sought to ensure sovereignty over their political, economic and cultural destinies. As a result, the very forces that were making the world more connected and homogenous were simultaneously triggering a powerful desire for local autonomy and preservation of unique cultural identity.... What we learned was something simple, yet powerful: that the next big evolutionary step of "going global" now has to be "going local...." We will not abandon the benefits of being global. But if our local colleagues develop an idea or strategy that is the right thing to do locally ... then they have the authority and responsibility to make it happen.... In our recent past, we succeeded because we understood and appealed to global commonalities. In our future, we'll succeed because we will also understand and appeal to local differences.[8]

So, even the management of Coca-Cola, in many ways the bellwether of all global brands, has recognized that if a brand is to connect with consumers at a meaningful level, it has to draw upon the everyday experience of those consumers for user imagery, aspects of personality, and message. At this level of culture, of course, consumers still differ significantly by country and even region within country, even though they are more aware of other cultures than in the past. Coca-Cola offers local brands such as Thums Up in India alongside its global house brand. It must be acknowledged that Daft's perspective is that of an executive in the extremely culture-bound food and drink category in which local variation in taste is pronounced, so the perspective of a business-to-business marketer would differ significantly. Nevertheless, he argues that the phenomena he observes apply more widely than just to the business of his company. In any sphere in which image or identity is important, he contends, customers will embrace the benefits of global standardization until those benefits are taken for granted, and they will then seek to emphasize their

---

8. Douglas Daft, "Back to Classic Coke," *Financial Times*, March 27, 2000, p. 15.

local culture. This is in line with the evolutionary view of global brand quality discussed earlier in this chapter, and it is also in line with trends in other image-oriented markets, in which it is quite common for fashionable or widely regarded brands to lose their appeal when an influential segment decides that they are too popular and seek something more distinctive with which to identify themselves.

It is worth noting that Daft stresses the company's continuing policy of seeking international economies of scale in marketing where possible. This is obviously going to require that Coca-Cola, as a brand, continues with its uniform name and visual identity. This allows Coca-Cola, as a company, to create promotional platforms that can be leveraged globally and that can be supported by international expenditures and promotional initiatives, yielding the desired economies of scale. As long as the promotions are restricted to name and visual identity, they can be used anywhere without restricting local execution in terms of message or imagery. In fact, Coca-Cola is a perfect example of how name and visual identity become merely a means of recognition and carry little meaning. The brand's name reflects the fact that its original formulation included cocaine (in days when attitudes to that substance were somewhat different). The company would surely have altered the name if consumers were drawing some meaning from it in the literal sense. The meaning they attach to the brand, rather, draws upon the nuanced detail of the execution of promotions for the brand. Consistency at the level of name and appearance will also satisfy the needs of retailers for international ordering and stock accounting and allow freedom for either in-store or extra-store promotion that is localized. So, the moves being made by companies such as Unilever and Procter & Gamble to reduce and standardize their global brand portfolio are not in conflict with this approach because they still offer the company the flexibility to localize at the level of positioning and meaning. McDonald's also illustrates this approach—the company maintains consistency in visual recognition with considerable variation at all levels, many at deeper levels of meaning. It is clear that in many multinationals, it is at this level that globalization of branding occurs most frequently: a survey of European brand managers, in which over 80 percent of respondents were found to be harmonizing their brand marketing across the region, investigated which elements of the marketing mix were most often globalized, and the two most globalized facets were the logotype/trademark (93 percent of respondents) and the brand names (81 percent), after which the next most commonly globalized element was product features with only 67 percent.[9]

ALLOW FOR EVOLUTION OF BRAND POSITION OVER TIME AND VARIATION IN DIFFERENT MARKETS

It is almost inevitable that a company participating in a variety of international markets will be following different strategies in different countries. Three factors produce this variation. First, consumer tastes evolve, as previously discussed. In particular, there appears to be variation in the extent to which national cultures value global versus local brands over time. Second, companies make deliberate decisions to vary their strategy from market to market—consistency of positioning is constrained by differences in marketing strategy adopted by companies or their national distributors. As was discussed in the previous chapter, internationalizing companies frequently enter new country-markets by aiming at the position they wished they had achieved in their domestic market. Most often, this means adopting a premium position in an attempt to skim the market. For example, Levi jeans or Timberland boots are valued in their domestic U.S. market for durability and toughness, are valued by segments such as students or construction site workers, and are priced in mid-market and positioned on their functional benefits; in international markets, by contrast, they are premium brands with a fashion positioning and an American aura. Similarly, mineral waters such as Perrier (from France) and San Pellegrino (from Italy) are positioned in international

---

9. Survey conducted by Kapferer/Eurocom and reported in Jean-Noel Kapferer, *Strategic Brand Management*, 2nd ed. (Dover, NH: Kogan Page, 1997): 361–372.

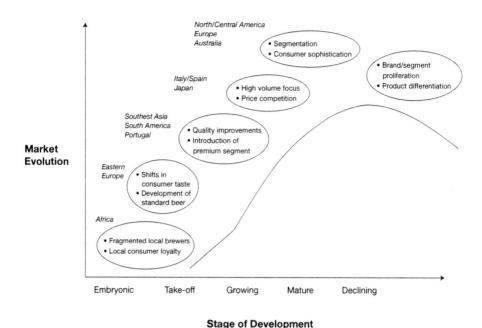

Stage of Development

FIGURE 4-3 Heineken: Beer Category Development by Country *(Source: Quelch, "Heineken N.V.: Global Advertising and Branding")*

markets as premium brands from countries with a reputation for style and taste.

Third, markets develop over time in more or less predictable ways, which experienced managers in certain product categories understand well. An example is shown in Figure 4–3, which describes Heineken's view of how countries develop in terms of their taste for beer.[10] In general terms, this follows a pattern that many managers would recognize of industry consolidation and the emergence of large brands, followed by increasing segmentation, fragmentation, and more sharply differentiated positions on the part of a greater number of brands. It should be clear that international branding policy needs to be flexible enough to accommodate differences both among markets and in the same

10. John A. Quelch, "Heineken N.V.: Global Advertising and Branding," Harvard Business School case study 9-596-015. Boston: Harvard Business School Publishing.

market over time. A globally consistent brand positioning, in which all elements of the marketing mix were the same in all markets, would clearly restrict Heineken's ability to meet these challenges. In general terms, it is essential that an international branding strategy is dynamic, retaining a core of consistency (as described in the previous section) but evolving to meet the different market conditions the brand will inevitably encounter.

SEPARATE BRAND POLICY FROM PRODUCT POLICY

A perfect example of how product and brand can be managed separately is provided by the managerial framework employed in the laundry detergent division of the German consumer product company Henkel (see Figure 4–4).[11] Henkel has internationalized over a long period largely through acquisition of local businesses, each time adding new factories and new brands to its portfolio, and so many of its brands are also distinctive product formulations (i.e., they are in the lower left-hand box of the quadrant). The company has decided that, even in this innovation-driven product category, it has more product variety than is required, and so over time it has been actively standardizing a number of products among countries and achieving production economies. It has recognized, however, that the brands it has acquired often have established local identities and loyal customer franchises, and so it resists standardization in this aspect of the marketing mix. What is described as the "product performance strategy" is therefore far more common in the company than the "brand platform strategy" (the latter is restricted to situations in which detailed consumer research justifies a shift in brand identity). In those few cases in which brand standardization is adopted, it is executed gradually, with name changes and new identities introduced incrementally in a series of small changes over a relatively long period of time.

---

11. David J. Arnold and Hans-Willi Schroiff, "Henkel KGaA Detergents Division: Global Branding Issues in the European Market," Harvard Business School case study 9-502-019. Boston: Harvard Business School Publishing. I am indebted to Dr. Hans-Willi Schroiff of Henkel and the Marketing Science Institute for their contribution to my thinking on global branding issues.

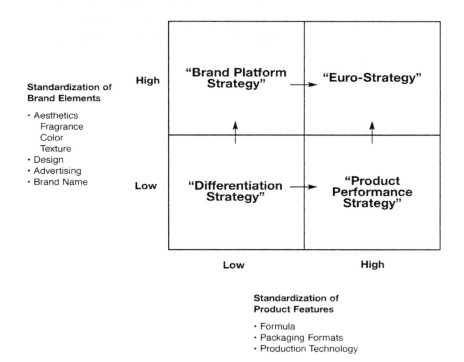

FIGURE 4–4 "Henkel Quadrant"—International Brand and Product Strategies *(Source: International Market Research, Henkel KGaA)*

ADOPT GLOBAL BRAND POLICIES FOR NEW BRANDS

Another interesting implication of the Henkel quadrant in Figure 4–4 is the prescription of global branding policies (described as "Euro strategy") for new brands or new products. While acknowledging the existence of variation in consumer preference and taste by country, it is also true that the most successful global brands are those that were introduced as such, particularly those that internationalized via an export strategy. Gillette's global introduction of new products and new brands, such as Sensor and Mach 3, illustrates how an innovative product is less constrained by existing patterns of taste.

There are two reasons why new brands are more suitable for global branding. First, many of the constraints on global branding from local variation in taste are actually the constraint of habit or familiarity rather than a preference for the local brand *per se*. Consumers may prefer local brands if they perceive it to be closely linked to a local origin, but they otherwise have no reason to choose a brand because its availability is locally restricted—any more than they would choose a brand simply because it is globally available. Although global visibility plays a role, it must be emphasized that, from the consumer perspective, it is local presence that drives brand image, whereas global visibility (which in effect means awareness while traveling) is an optional extra for brand success. What is well-established is that consumers develop relationships with existing brands that run far deeper than whether the brand is local or global. Given that global brands are a relatively recent phenomenon and that most brand consumption is of local brands, a consumer is being asked to break an established habit or relationship when being asked to subscribe to a global brand (except in those few cases, such as luxury goods, in which globalism is associated with prestige positioning that enhances brand value). Indeed, it is consumers' preference for their established repertoire of brands rather than preference for either local or global brands that may represent the greatest challenge companies face in undertaking brand harmonization initiatives. However, this clearly does not apply in the case of new brands, which can be designed to have international appeal (regarding, for example, the name of the brand) and can be launched to achieve many of the benefits of global branding already described.

A second opportunity for establishing new global brands is when an innovative product is launched. Although product and brand can be managed separately, of course, the launch of an innovative product will frequently be executed under a new brand. While adaptations or improved versions of existing products will be linked with their preceding product versions, and so be constrained by the inherited brand image, products that represent a new concept in the market operate in a green field, as regards consumer perceptions. This distinction has been described as "Disruption vs. Optimization Marketing" by French branding professor Jean-Noel Kapferer, who comments that "strong innovation ... that which conveys new vision, tends to impose itself on all countries and hardly needs any adapting."[12] Again, without the constraint of existing brand perceptions, the company can design a globally acceptable brand and reap some of the benefits of global branding without running against ingrained consumer preference structures. This may also apply to innovative extensions of existing brands, such as the extension of Mars into ice cream or Swatch into sunglasses.

INSTITUTE A "BUY GLOBALLY, SELL LOCALLY" ORGANIZATIONAL MODEL

For a company to balance global efficiency with local responsiveness, there must exist a marketing organization structure that can coordinate among markets in supporting the global brand name and then pass on these platforms to local marketing units to execute with a degree of localization. A model of such an organization is provided by the example of Master-Card's sponsorship of the soccer World Cup.[13] MasterCard is a global franchise without any direct contact with its end users, competing against other franchises within its member banks, by which it is owned. The approach adopted by MasterCard is to invest in a marketing communications program (the World Cup sponsorship) at the corporate level, and then offer its operating units (the member banks) great flexibility in their use of this platform. MasterCard designs and distributes a large number of potential promotional ideas, such as competitions with match tickets as prizes, ideas for events featuring prominent soccer stars, and a range of literature. These "kits" are sent out to member banks, but MasterCard cannot exert influence over

---

12. Jean-Noel Kapferer, *Strategic Brand Management*, 2nd ed. (Dover, NH: Kogan Page, 1997), 352.

13. David Lane and David J. Arnold, "MasterCard International: World Championship Soccer Sponsorship," Harvard Business School case study 9-500-036. Boston: Harvard Business School Publishing.

which (if any) will be used. Local banks can, of course, initiate their own promotions, but they have an incentive to adopt those produced by MasterCard because design costs are already covered. Moreover, the benefits of the promotions accrue at the local level (i.e., the member banks), even though it is the corporate center (MasterCard) that has invested in the marketing platform of the sponsorship.

MasterCard has therefore achieved a balance between global integration and local adaptation based upon a recognition that the size and global appeal of the World Cup constitute a force strong enough to add value to its relatively locally oriented member banks. As regards economies of scale from global expenditure in a marketing platform,

- MasterCard has the scale to afford a global brand program such as the World Cup sponsorship. An individual bank could never undertake this sponsorship alone.
- Conversely, MasterCard needs global roll-out to cover the fixed cost of the sponsorship. This is a sound basis for the sponsorship partnership.
- It is important to note that the World Cup is more than simply a vehicle for the promotion of global brands—it is a global brand in itself (i.e., it has wide global awareness and distribution, a consistent visual identity, and a universal meaning and relevance). Indeed, when compared with many product or service brands, it is clear that the World Cup is one of the world's most powerful and most global brands. Each World Cup finals tournament has its own logo and visual identity, incorporating the year and the venue as well as a unique design. As such, it provides a perfect partner for a brand seeking to strengthen its global position, such as MasterCard.

With regard to facilitating localization of the sponsorship property, MasterCard has leveraged the sponsorship with great adroitness:

- Its core approach, and a vital ingredient of the sponsorship's success, was the strategy of offering member banks a "toolkit" and thus offering them the ability to design turnkey programs rather than designing a more restricted promotions program and trying to obtain buy-in. From the member banks' perspective, there is little coercion to resist and a menu of marketing possibilities from which to choose.

- In financial terms, MasterCard not only funded the capital cost of the sponsorship by contracting for the sponsorship, but also organized regional contributions and extra promotional investments, to the tune of at least the industry average of 200–300 percent of the actual sponsorship contract cost. This created a remarkable multiplier effect (member banks spending far more than MasterCard), which shows a superb return on investment for a marketing program.

- MasterCard undertook an integrated communications program attempting to encourage synergies among member banks and other participating sponsors, organizing exclusivities for event-related marketing, integrating promotions with wider campaigns, and actively managing the threat of ambush marketing.

- MasterCard also established opportunities for knowledge transfer through manuals, case studies, and other communications programs designed to maximize the benefits to a member bank that was part of the sponsorship.

The conceptual point here is that MasterCard has designed a very effective system for managing the corporate global marketing role in a marketing system consisting of many powerful locally-oriented units. The following are key elements:

- MasterCard bears the initial investment cost.
- MasterCard attempts to provide incentives to member banks to invest further rather than demanding contributions.
- MasterCard allows returns on the investment to accrue at the local level.
- MasterCard restricts its own role to areas in which its central position in the marketing system adds clear value (e.g., scale, the creation of communications networks, and the management of relationships with other parties in the system, which includes other sponsors and event organizers).

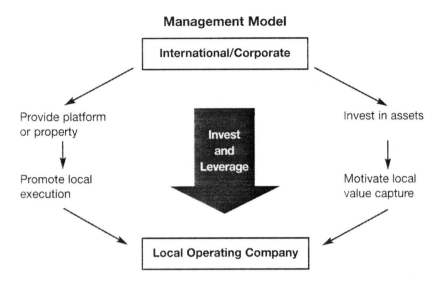

FIGURE 4–5   MasterCard: Organizational Model for Global Brand Promotion

The key elements of this model are illustrated in Figure 4–5. This model requires a separation of management of core marketing platforms that can be attached to the core brand elements of name and appearance from management of promotional positionings that add local detail to this core brand identity. It also requires a separation of investment, undertaken at the corporate center, from returns, which are allowed to accrue to the benefit of local units. Such operating models, while still rare, are increasing—a few multinationals follow a similar approach in investing in TV program formats, which can then be rolled out worldwide (with the format being adapted if necessary), to be used locally in bargaining large deals with local media for airtime.

SUMMARY

Consumers demand global brands far less than many companies imagine. Indeed, it is globalizing companies that stand to benefit more from global brands than any global consumers who might exist. There is little evidence to alter the fundamental principle of marketing that consumers choose brands according to their perceived value relative to their needs and then stick with them until the emergence of any contrary evidence. Nevertheless, it is clear that, absent of brand heritage or ingrained consumption patterns, an international corporation would seek brand harmonization, as for example when launching new brands, since there are considerable managerial economies or economies of control to be gained. It can also be reasonably supposed that, in the future, we shall see international consolidation in retail and marketing expenditure, areas in which to date most consolidation has been within national borders. There is no reason to suspect that this will alter basic consumer dynamics in established categories, however, and so global brands will continue to offer added value to consumers from their globalism per se in a restricted number of product areas, such as luxury or high-technology products.

Critical issues discussed in this chapter include the following:

- The identification of genuine benefits to marketing companies from global brand harmonization, especially in aspects of the marketing infrastructure such as retail distribution and international event-related promotion.

- The distinction between a brand name and a brand meaning (or positioning). Global recognition of name and visual identity can be sought while still recognizing and allowing localization of brand meaning. In effect, the brand's overall identity can be disaggregated into hierarchical levels of benefit bundles, some of which offer returns to global scale (e.g., universal recognition) while others offer returns to localization (e.g., brand personality and meaning).

- Many "global brands" are in fact national brands (associated with their country of origin) that have achieved global distribution and recognition.

- There is a vital distinction between a product and a brand, and in some industries, these two decision fields can be managed independently of each other (e.g., the product can be globally consistent, even if the brand personality is different, and vice versa).

■ Enlightened corporate management of globally distributed brands may involve investment in a menu of brand promotional tools, all conforming to a broad set of brand principles, while allowing local flexibility in execution.

5 SELECTING AND MANAGING INTERNATIONAL DISTRIBUTORS

Many executives refer to the challenge of "achieving international distribution" when discussing their firm's international development. They are right to make distribution synonymous with internationalization, since it remains the greatest challenge in the establishment of an international marketing network. Whereas international companies can enter new markets by leveraging existing assets such as product portfolios and operations networks, they have to start from scratch in sales and distribution because market systems remain nationally regulated and dominated by complex networks of local intermediaries. Even the largest multinational corporations frequently remain dependent upon a local distribution partner to gain market access, as discussed in Chapter 3, and in many cases they are legally obliged to operate with a local partner holding at least a 50 percent equity stake at the time of entry. Although a few of the largest multinationals have established their own distribution channels soon after market entry (examples include Procter & Gamble and Coca-Cola in Eastern Europe), a contract with a local third-party agent or distributor remains the "dominant design" for market participation in the early stages. With the establishment of more than 30 new nation states since 1990, along with the liberalization of several other high-potential country-markets, multinationals continue to struggle with the challenge of building distribution in international markets. While the range of possible entry modes, such as import agents or franchisees, was reviewed in Chapter 3, this chapter will focus on this dominant form of market participation—the appointment of a local independent organization as a national agent and distributor.

It is this partnership with a local distributor, and its perceived underperformance, that is identified by many MNCs as the major obstacle to sustained growth after the market entry phase. As a result, the dominant pattern of internationalization has come to be what is sometimes labeled the "increasing commitment" strategy: after entering the market via an independent local distributor, the MNC switches to direct distribution by reacquiring the distribution rights (or, in some cases, by buying the distributor company) and establishing a directly owned and controlled subsidiary. Open the business press almost any week, and it will contain reports of MNCs increasing their investment in and control over international distribution in order to develop further their international marketing network. Talk to executives in these companies, and they will often portray the "typical distributor" as a necessary partner at the market entry stage but as a wholly inadequate partner for long-run market development due to its lack of marketing capability.

In fact, the truth has as much to do with low managerial standards in the MNCs as with the shortcomings of national distributors. Many international companies, which operate complex and sophisticated distributor control systems in their domestic markets, are content to leave their international business to sink or swim in the hands of distributors who do not benefit from these managerial systems or processes. Moreover, while the increasing commitment strategy may be optimal overall, the transition from distributor to subsidiary is at best disruptive to business and is frequently disputatious if the local distributor decides to contest or resist the takeover.

This chapter will firstly describe the typical life cycle of the international distribution relationship, and it will then diagnose the underlying factors causing this evolution. This forms the basis for managerial guidelines for overcoming the frustrations of managing international distribution.[1]

THE INTERNATIONAL DISTRIBUTION LIFE CYCLE

The typical pattern through which international distribution passes is shown in Figure 5–1. The key dimension is ownership of the distribution channel. Initially, MNCs generally choose (and are sometimes required by local regulation) to go to market through a local, independently owned distribution company. This distributor is usually (but not always) granted territorial exclusivity (i.e., it is the sole authorized distributor in the country or region). This arrangement is regarded by international distributors as standard practice, and it will certainly be requested by any distributor candidates, the justification being that it is required in order to encourage them to invest in business development without the risk of another distributor free-riding on that investment. The distributor buys product from the MNC and then markets the product within its territory. From the MNC's perspective, therefore, this can frequently be regarded as a financially marginal activity, incurring no extra fixed costs and minimal risk, most of which are borne by the local distributor.

This arrangement rarely lasts, however. In over ten years of researching in this area, I have heard more times than I can remember something like the following archetypal account of international distribution:

> We have usually found that sales grow well in the first few years after entry, but then begin to slow and, in many cases, plateau. In our early years, we were slow to take action because most of our focus was on the U.S. market and not on the international market. Then we began to try various

1. David J. Arnold, "Seven Rules of International Distribution," *Harvard Business Review*, November–December 2000.

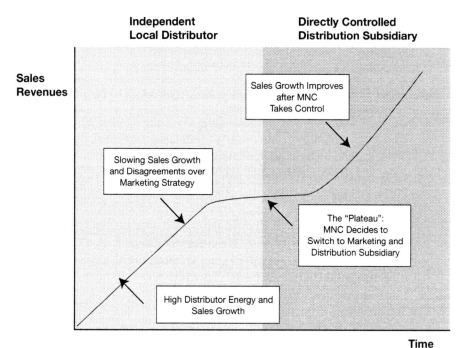

FIGURE 5–1 The International Distributor Life Cycle

initiatives to remedy the slowdown, including switching product lines, changing prices, or even putting one of our managers into the market, but generally with little effect. What has invariably happened has been that we decide to take over the distribution operation ourselves. It remains a difficult ride, however. At best, the decision to take control of distribution ourselves leads to long negotiations over acquisition of the distributor company or our franchise, during which business is disrupted. At worst, we have ended up in long legal battles and have had distributors steal our technology and set up in competition, or dump inventory into the market to make it impossible for us to continue our own business profitably. When we try to figure out what we have learned, we can't decide whether we picked the wrong distributor, or whether we exercised too much control or too little. In the end, we always do a better job with our subsidiary, and this is the model we prefer because of the greater control we get. But we still need a local distributor for entry, and we are still searching for a strategy to get us through the transition without battles over control and performance.

These disputes with national distributors always involve general accusations of underperformance by the distributor, frequently more specific grievances such as underpricing in order to move inventory, and sometimes more serious offenses such as complicity in manufacture of counterfeit product or selling in neighboring territories outside the distributor's designated area. From the distributor's perspective, there are general accusations of "betrayal" of the partnership by the MNC and more specific grievances such as failure to supply product. Even when the distributor is made aware of the likelihood of the MNC wishing to take back control of distribution after a few years in market, those few years are sufficient to change its mind about whether it wishes to hang on to the business. And, of course, regulatory regimes usually favor the local company over a multinational. The result is a significant proportion of relationships that end in dispute, whether in the courts or outside. Indeed, in many multinationals, primary responsibility for managing international distribution rests with the legal department, a symptom of the contentious nature of many such relationships.

This particular account was related by David Freeman, CEO of Loctite, the adhesives and specialty chemicals group that is now part of the German company Henkel and that was long widely admired for its international distribution network.[2] As in this case, the problem is often characterized as primarily one of control, to which the solution is majority or total ownership of the sales and distribution operation. Like Loctite, most MNCs had first followed this strategy in a series of unplanned remedial moves that were based on case-by-case judgments on how to reinvigorate their business in a number

2.   David J. Arnold and John A. Quelch, "Loctite Corporation: International Distribution," Harvard Business School case study 9-549-021. Boston: Harvard Business School Publishing.

of markets. As the pattern recurred, this stepwise approach to market entry and penetration was adopted as Loctite's strategy for internationalization. As a result, the company now undertakes more market entries than earlier in its history, and it passes more rapidly through the first phase of independent local distribution, facilitated by contracts that give it the option to buy back its distribution rights after a few years in market. The received wisdom underlying the strategy is that the local distributor is best viewed as a market entry vehicle— a temporary partner that can introduce the new entrant to the market, but cannot sustain growth over the longer term.

For all these reasons, most MNCs adopt the increasing commitment strategy to market penetration and development. On the face of it, this strategy makes sense. The distributor is an indispensable partner for market entry because the MNC alone cannot master local business practices, meet regulatory requirements, hire and manage local personnel, and gain introductions to potential customers. But, in the long run, most MNCs want to control their own operations through a directly owned subsidiary. This is not only because of the economies of scale and control obtainable across a global network of marketing operations but, more fundamentally, because most companies believe that no independent partner could match their own focus and product knowledge and therefore their ability to grow the business. Very rarely indeed does an MNC switch to another distributor rather than set up its own direct sales subsidiary. Moreover, in almost all cases, the switch from independent to direct distribution is validated by the sales curve: the switch is often made in response to a slowdown in sales performance, and growth is resumed after the MNC takes control.

In practice, this evolution remains problematic for two principal reasons. First, there are the disruptions or disputes already described. Second, by repeatedly replacing distributors with company-owned subsidiaries, the MNCs are sacrificing the potential efficiencies of distributors and risk overinvestment in intensive organizational networks in areas that could be handled at a supranational level, such as Western Europe. An alternative way of thinking about this is to consider the international distribution life cycle (Figure 5–1) in terms of profit rather than sales growth; although sales growth almost invariably surges after the switch to direct distribution, we should remember that costs or investments surge too, as the MNC builds its own organization in market and invests in marketing programs. Most MNCs simply do not know whether the extra sales exceed the extra costs because they never knew for sure the former distributor's costs, but it is quite possible that in many cases profits decline, at least in the short term. There are economic reasons for the existence of distributors; the economies of scope resulting from carrying a number of vendors' product lines result in more efficient distribution than any one company could achieve alone. Ironically, many MNCs understand and operationalize this in their domestic markets, but they fail to apply the same managerial insight in international markets.

Third, the new situation can also create new problems. Once a local distributor knows that the business is likely to be bought back after a number of years, its incentives are to maximize the measures by which the business will be valued rather than to undertake long-term business development. The Asia-Pacific manager of a consumer goods company reported that several national distributors, acting in the belief that sales revenues were the key to the reacquisition price, had cut prices, boosting overall revenues but undermining the company's market positioning strategies. Ironically, two European distributors for the same company had adopted premium pricing, happy to turn the business into a niche player in order to boost the gross margin that they thought critical to valuation.

What can MNCs do to avoid the distributor crisis? Although MNCs attribute the need to change strategy to the inadequacies of local distributors, there is plenty they can do to manage better the process of market development. In particular, it is vital to understand the differences between the role of a distributor in the domestic and international markets. Until now, most MNCs appoint as international distributors the same type of partner they use at home and then manage them less rigorously. The regional manager for a consumer durable corporation observed that distributors know the market, and since corporations don't have the information to make detailed judgments on what the distributors are doing, the corporations tend to leave them alone and instead focus on counting sales revenues. The more experienced MNCs are adapting their approach, however, based upon too many years of living through the distributor crisis.

THE DISTRIBUTOR CRISIS

The distributor crisis, in which the MNC decides that it must take control in order to achieve sustained sales growth, is a window into the dynamics of international distribution. Unsurprisingly, MNCs and local distributors offer different interpretations of the crisis. MNCs generally point to underperformance (in particular to slowing sales growth) as the key issue. In some cases, they identify a more specific target that has not been met, such as sales of a newly introduced product or penetration of a new region or city within the country. By contrast, distributors tend to attribute the crisis to the MNC's organizational shortcomings, specifying factors such as lack of vendor support, technical advice, samples, or even product delivery. Also widely cited but vaguer in character is the distributor theory that ascribes the takeover of distribution to "politics," such as the MNC's desire to capture the distributor's revenue in its own income statement, a more general desire for control, or "empire-building" on the part of some of its executives that led them to invest in distribution operations regardless of the market circumstances.

It is clear that both parties in the relationship contribute to the way in which it evolves, and the distributor relationship is often outgrown by the changing business situation. Thus, the very qualities that make the distributor an attractive partner for market entry, such as a local focus and a strong existing customer base, later become a handicap. Moreover, both MNCs and distributors grow to expect the pattern to repeat itself, which in some cases results in the independent distributor managing the agency to maximize buy-out value in the medium term rather than to establish the best platform for long-run market leadership. The increasing commitment pattern may thus become a self-fulfilling prophecy.

The big lesson here lies in understanding the changing nature of the business situation that the relationship is designed to address. Better management of the relationship in this context of change can lead to improved performance in international markets and mitigate or avoid the frustrations so common in this field. To begin with, it is important to identify the three most common business performance issues that sabotage the relationship.

LACK OF STRATEGIC MARKETING

In many cases, argue an MNC's executives, the satisfactory initial sales growth has been achieved by "picking the low-hanging fruit"—relatively easy sales of the MNC's proven core products to its distributor's existing customer base. The sales plateau occurs when this entry platform can no longer support growth, and the key business challenge shifts to objectives such as introducing additional products from the multinational's range or penetrating new market segments in which the distributor is not established. Distributors are viewed as closely tied to a fixed customer base, to which they distribute a relatively narrow and unchanging range of products. While this is attractive at the point of market entry because it accelerates the establishment of the business in the country, it becomes an obstacle when the saturation of this core market demands strategic product and market development initiatives. One executive said that distributors tend to be good at selling, but they have no clue when some marketing is required.

LACK OF INVESTMENT IN BUSINESS GROWTH

Although distributors are often granted national exclusivity in order to encourage investment in business development and although contracts sometimes stipulate minimum levels of marketing investments (expressed as percentage of sales revenues), a lack of investment is repeatedly cited as a source of dissatisfaction. This interpretation of events is often accompanied by comments on the "typical distributor," such as "a trader," which is generally thought to have decision makers who think in terms of working capital rather than in terms of investments and returns, or who will do deals that others wouldn't just to keep product moving out of the door. It is supported by the repeated experience of healthy returns on the increased investment typically made by MNCs after the switch to their own sales subsidiary. It is also clear that this issue appears to grow more salient over time as an MNC builds up a record of buying out its national distribution operations after a number of years in market, thus creating an expectation of a limited-term partnership. A limited number of MNC executives acknowledge the distributor view that they themselves underinvest in supporting the local partner's efforts to build the business, which is attributed to risk minimization or, more simply, "lazy management."

LACK OF AMBITION BY THE DISTRIBUTOR

In some cases, this growth plateau was attributed to a lack of "drive to dominate the market." To paraphrase many MNC managers, the typical distributor is not looking for market domination, but for a stable mid-sized business that makes the owner-managers wealthy but is not too big for them to control personally. This reflects the fact that in many countries distribution organizations are privately owned, and that MNCs often select this type of partner. Specific problems reported included conflicts of interest within the distributor between the MNC's product lines and those of a competitor, or the principal's lack of motivation to grow its organization beyond a certain size. In such cases, the desire for aggressive growth is either absent or wanes after a few years. The distributor's desire for autonomy may also be reflected by an unwillingness to grow too dependent upon one manufacturer.

These problems are symptoms of a wider issue—the fact that distributors play a different role in international markets. In general, MNCs do not expect their domestic distributors to possess high-level strategic marketing capability, and they see it as their own responsibility to set stretch goals for market domination. Yet, in international markets, they tend to recruit partners close to the domestic distributor profile on the grounds that these are the companies that are serving the most obvious customers with the most closely related product range. An understanding of the differences in distribution strategy in domestic and international markets is the first step in designing better relationships with international distributors.

DISTRIBUTION IS DIFFERENT IN INTERNATIONAL MARKETS

In the management of distribution strategy, perhaps more than any other area of marketing, there are significant differences between practice in the international and domestic market contexts. The fundamental reason for the challenges of the international distributor life cycle are these differences, which are generally little understood. The following should help to clarify these differences:

A WIDER RANGE OF FUNCTIONS DEMANDED OF THE DISTRIBUTOR

A national distributor for an international corporation is generally responsible not just for the conventional distribution functions,[3] but also for marketing strategy functions for the country-market. The "distributor" is the *de facto* branch or marketing company of the MNC in that country for two reasons. First, the distributor will usually have been granted an

---

3. Usually defined as carrying inventory, demand generation, physical distribution, after-sales service, and financing customer accounts.

exclusive agency for the market—even this is never done in the domestic market. This expanded responsibility is granted in order to encourage investment in market development, and it also provides easier accountability from the MNC's perspective. Second, MNCs are generally concerned to minimize their risk during the market entry phase, and they therefore commit fewer resources to building their business than would be the case at home, delegating this instead to their local partner. Although these two factors call for a local partner with the marketing capability to build a market from scratch, MNCs frequently select partners more akin to traditional distributors in terms of skill set and business philosophy, and it is their lack of strategic marketing capability that prompts the MNCs to switch to a directly owned distribution subsidiary.

RAPID GROWTH OF BUSINESS

International markets are characterized by a faster and more conscious evolution through the growth curve of business development than in the "first-time-around" domestic market. The evolution, from low-commitment market entry through local business development to consolidation into a global network, accelerates with international experience, from a more laissez-faire attitude in early years of international operation to a deliberate and more forceful approach as the firm attaches greater importance to its international business. If the distributor partnership is to last, therefore, it must involve a distributor organization that can not only meet the market entry objectives, but can also grow with the business and contribute to the business development initiatives that will be required to develop business beyond the entry platform. In many cases, MNCs contract with distributors unable to adapt to these relatively rapid changes in business objectives but still expect them to build their business over the long run.

MULTIMARKET DECISIONS

Once a firm is operating in several country-markets, it inevitably starts comparing them in terms of performance and transferring policies, products, and people among them. The result is that decisions are made on the basis of system optimization rather than market optimization or simply in the belief that what was learned in one market is transferable to another. This explains the distributor perspective that MNCs were making decisions for their own internal reasons rather than responding to the market. Given that MNCs tend not to have detailed market and financial data regarding the distributor's performance, they may evaluate distributors not on the same quantitative criteria used in the home market, but on the basis of mental models of business growth transferred from other markets ("market entry mode" or "investment phase") or on the corporate "distribution culture" of preferring to deal primarily with either distributors or subsidiaries.

The key to understanding the distinctive challenges of international distribution is to take an evolutionary perspective. The shape of the challenge is described in Figure 5–2. As the business grows in an international market, marketing strategy evolves through a series of phases, each requiring additional management resources, new skills, and financial investment.[4] The fit between the MNC's product line and the distributor's business is probably best at the point of market entry, and it declines over time as product and market developments are undertaken. The distributor may be less able to deliver sales growth as the business moves away from its core base. Moreover, the investment required may seem less attractive to a distributor than taking on another vendor and "picking the low-hanging fruit" over again.

Seen in this context, the underlying problems in managing international distributors take on a new light. It is not enough to say that local distributors lack marketing capability or fail to invest enough in aggressive business development plans. The underlying problem is that *nobody is performing these functions*—even though they are necessary for business growth.

---

4. See Susan P. Douglas and C. Samuel Craig, "Evolution of Global Marketing Strategy: Scale, Scope, and Synergy," *Columbia Journal of World Business* (Fall 1989), and the discussion of this framework in Chapter 3.

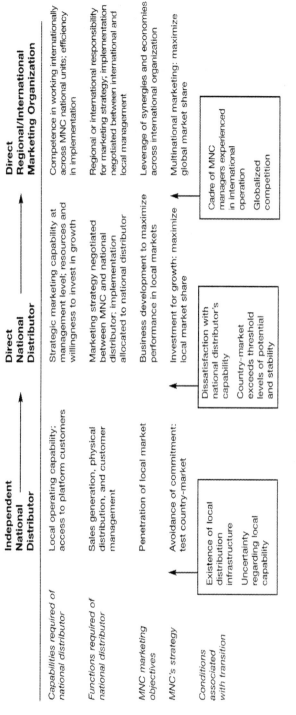

	Independent National Distributor	Direct National Distributor	Direct Regional/International Marketing Organization
Capabilities required of national distributor	Local operating capability; access to platform customers	Strategic marketing capability at management level; resources and willingness to invest in growth	Competence in working internationally across MNC national units; efficiency in implementation
Functions required of national distributor	Sales generation, physical distribution, and customer management	Marketing strategy negotiated between MNC and national distributor; implementation allocated to national distributor	Regional or international responsibility for marketing strategy; implementation negotiated between international and local management
MNC marketing objectives	Penetration of local market	Business development to maximize performance in local markets	Leverage of synergies and economies across international organization
MNC's strategy	Avoidance of commitment: test country-market	Investment for growth: maximize local market share	Multinational marketing: maximize global market share
Conditions associated with transition	Existence of local distribution infrastructure Uncertainty regarding local capability	Dissatisfaction with national distributor's capability Country-market exceeds threshold levels of potential and stability	Cadre of MNC managers experienced in international operation Globalized competition

FIGURE 5–2 The Evolving Challenge of International Distribution

More simply, nobody is doing the marketing. Large corporations, which have learned the necessity of a marketing function as a pilot for sales activity, nevertheless frequently tolerate unguided sales partners as the vanguard of their international marketing effort. Although it may be rational for MNCs to minimize their risk when entering new markets, the resulting lack of investment and managerial attention can seriously hamper performance, given the need to build a market from scratch. If the local partner chosen is close to the profile of a traditional distributor from the domestic market and is qualified to perform only the traditional distribution functions, it is unlikely to possess the marketing capability required and is unlikely to be willing and/or able to invest in the growth of a business in which the MNC is minimizing its commitment.

GUIDELINES FOR MANAGING THE INTERNATIONAL DISTRIBUTOR LIFE CYCLE

This imbalance between business objectives and the expectations and capabilities of the two partners is the major factor underlying the problems of the international distributor life cycle, and managerial guidelines emerge from the consistent patterns of imbalance and corrections that result. The sequence of decisions involved is a series of trade-offs among three objectives (see Figure 5–3). First, all MNCs have to understand the importance of controlling their international business at the strategic level, whatever the arrangement employed for local implementation.

Such control enhances performance (through leverage of the corporation's global strengths) and is also necessary to ensure a degree of consistency of marketing strategy among country-markets. Second, all corporations need to contract representation by local nationals because of the distinctive local character of most market systems, and because most customers prefer a local face. This is particularly important in the first years in a new country-market, when local operat-

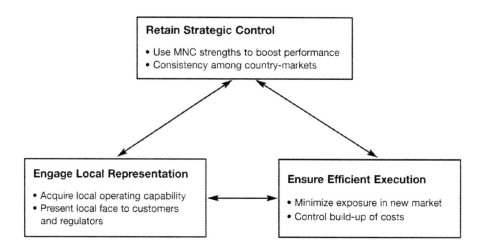

FIGURE 5-3 The Trade-Offs of Managing International Distribution

ing capability can be achieved only through representation by local managers. Third, all MNCs are quite rationally concerned that the benefits of growth through internationalization are not jeopardized by an accumulation of new costs or exposure to avoidable risks.

Many of the changes made during internationalization, including the switch to directly controlled distribution, are corrective moves to redress imbalances in these trade-offs. In many cases, for instance, strategic control has been sacrificed at market entry in order to minimize the MNC's exposure in a new and uncertain environment. In the short-term, this results in the sales growth plateau and the consequent distributor crisis. One certain benefit of the switch is that the international firm will have ensured access to market and financial data that are essential to effective marketing management. However, the regaining of control through a switch to a directly-owned distribution subsidiary may, in the longer run, lead to a dense network of national distribution organizations that is judged inefficient relative to the potential economies of a regional marketing organization.

There are a number of guidelines that MNC executives should follow to minimize the disruption to business over the course of the international distributor life cycle.

RETAIN RESPONSIBILITY FOR MARKETING STRATEGY FROM MARKET ENTRY ONWARDS

The delegation of all marketing strategy functions to independent national distributors may lead to two sorts of problems. First, it demands of distributor organization capabilities that many do not possess, resulting in underperformance. Second, it allows inconsistencies in strategic positioning among country-markets, which the MNC will inevitably need to correct later as it globalizes its marketing. The full potential of a global marketing network can only be realized if strategic control of the business is retained in all country-markets, whatever their stage of evolution. Within the business template controlled by the MNC, independent distributors may be involved in local strategy adaptation as appropriate, and their local market intelligence will certainly be valuable. But it must be the MNC vendor that agrees to the marketing strategy, convenes and leads planning sessions, and has authority over decisions in areas such as positioning, budgeting, and product policy. This represents a significant change to the way most MNCs deal with independent distributors in international markets.

COMMIT MNC RESOURCES TO SUPPORTING MARKET ENTRY

Retention of strategic control requires the commitment of corporate resources even at market entry, the point of greatest uncertainty. For many internationalizing firms, such commitment represents unacceptable exposure, given the uncertainty of the new country-market and the fact that the distribution organization is independently owned. Experienced MNCs commit resources earlier in the process of market penetration for two reasons. First, commitment of resources by the MNC improves the quality of the relationship with the local distributor and thus enhances business performance. Second, the MNC learns that increased commitment is almost invariably the outcome of the "test market" period of market entry in any case: almost no instances have been encountered of MNCs withdrawing from countries they had entered (but only from distribution partnerships that had not been successful). To bring forward some of the investment is therefore an adaptation of strategy rather than a different approach, and it is one that will increase the MNC's control over the outcome. Although they are often not deployed in international markets, most MNCs have in their home market well-developed control systems for the management of independent distributors.

CHOOSE A DISTRIBUTOR AND STRUCTURE THE RELATIONSHIP ACCORDING TO CLEAR PARTNERSHIP GOALS

When entering a new market, it is essential for an MNC to synchronize the goals of the distribution strategy, the type of distributor selected, and the terms of the relationship. International companies most usually choose a distributor on the basis of market fit (i.e., they select the distributor most suited to reaching the most likely part of the market to produce initial sales). For example, the most appropriate type of distributor for fast market penetration may be one embedded in the local industry—possibly carrying competitor lines or even a manufacturer in its own right—and with a strong local focus. While there is an obviously valid logic behind this policy (a better chance of market penetration), it should always be recognized that in the medium term such a partner is likely to have conflicts of interest. These may arise directly from the competitor lines carried by the distributor or, more generally, from their desire to control the sector in the local market and thus prevent any one vendor from becoming dominant. In fact, this is often the dynamic that leads to the sales plateau in the international distributor life cycle.

MNCs should also consider selecting distributors on the basis of company fit: does the distributor organization demonstrate the culture and capabilities suitable for a long-term partnership even if it may lack the customer base necessary for fast establishment of the entry platform? Increasingly, the more sophisticated and experienced MNCs are including in their distributor candidates pools companies that have little experience in the relevant industry sector but that are prepared to invest in the MNCs' business in a committed and cooperative way. One way in which this sort of commitment would be evident is the distributor's willingness to reciprocate exclusivity (i.e., it undertakes not to sell any competitor products in exchange for territorial exclusivity). This is very different from the traditional distributor relationship (characterized by a mix of competition and cooperation), in which the distributor seeks as much control as possible over the local business, will not reveal customers' names or prices paid, and plays different vendors off against each other. A distributor chosen on the basis of company fit will be more likely to allow the MNC to retain strategic control, as previously mentioned, or to give the MNC access to financial and market data (see next section).

ENSURE ACCESS TO DETAILED MARKET AND FINANCIAL PERFORMANCE DATA

An MNC's ability to exploit its competitive advantages in any individual country-market depends heavily on the quality of information it obtains from that market. In many country-markets, the distribution organization is the only possible source of such information, and it is essential that the distribution contract requires the provision of detailed market and financial performance data. Such information is the basis of the MNC's control of its business and of the international leverage that constitutes one of the MNC's principal advantages. As previously mentioned, this arrangement is not traditionally accepted by distributors, and most can be counted on to resist the suggestion. Nevertheless, the bargaining power generally lies with the MNC. Moreover, the willingness of potential distributors to agree to provide such information was regarded by several MNC interviewees as a key early indicator of their approach to the relationship.

BUILD LINKS AMONG NATIONAL DISTRIBUTORS AT THE EARLIEST POSSIBLE OPPORTUNITY

While the primary focus after market entry is to build a customer base in the specific country-market, it is beneficial to build links among national distributors as early as possible. These links may take the form of a regional corporate office or an independent network such as a distributor council. The transfer of ideas among country-markets can improve performance and result in a greater degree of international consistency in the execution of strategies. The establishment of such links is an example of the modest commitment that is almost inevitable anyway, but which if implemented sooner can significantly improve the development of business in an international market.

These policies are already being followed in more experienced MNCs. Already established in most of the world's developed economies, these companies are entering emerging markets, with particular attention paid to the high-potential countries such as China, India, and Russia. It is clear that in these cases, the more-experienced MNCs attempt to exercise closer control over marketing strategy from the outset through mechanisms such as the secondment of employees to distributor organizations, minority stakes in the distributor organization, or the establishment of separate country managers either in market or in a regional office. They adopt an evolutionary perspective, drawing on their vision of a future global marketing network in which strategic marketing management responsibility is placed at the supranational (regional or global) level along with production, research, and physical distribution operations, while sales and customer service remain locally focused. Most international distribution channels appear to evolve, however, with strategic marketing and sales force implementation vested together in a single national operation. The involvement in marketing strategy from the outset of the relationship represents an unbundling of these functions, with the result that the national distributor is from the outset much closer to the *executor* of marketing strategy that it will eventually become.

LOOKING AHEAD—IS THERE A FUTURE FOR LOCAL DISTRIBUTORS?

This chapter has for the most part adopted the perspective of the international corporation, but there is another side to this particular topic, given its base in interorganizational relationships. From the perspective of a nationally oriented distributor, the trends discussed in this chapter are alarming. For some decades, international companies have followed the increasing commitment strategy to the point at which the very existence of local distributors seems under threat. Time and time again, employees of local distributors are lured into the MNC's new subsidiary by the prospects of higher pay or a career in an exciting and large international company. As I have frequently encountered in my research in this area, many cultures regard the increasing commitment strategy as inherently treacherous, given its instrumental perspective on business relationships. In addition, the prosperous survival of local distributors is an issue of concern to local politicians and others concerned with the globalization of markets. This all raises the question of whether the trend is irreversible or whether there is a future for local distribution organizations.

Instances of independent distributors surviving as the long-run representatives of MNCs are few. These outliers appear to display the following characteristics:

■ They are not in "strategic" countries where the MNC feels it has to have its own subsidiary irrespective of the quality of any local distributor. Such countries are variously defined as country-markets with high volume potential, regarded as "regional centers of gravity," or seen as suitable locations for operations such as manufacturing, research, or logistics centers.

■ These are not traditional, established distributor firms. Instead, these are often companies (or units of companies) that are new to the MNCs' business and have been selected on the basis of company fit rather than market fit. Executives in these distributor firms display higher levels of integration with the MNC, and as a result, the distributor organization grows up with the MNC's business in its market. Behaviors characteristic of this managerial approach include initiating joint business development projects with distributors in neighboring countries, submitting proposals to the MNC for business development initiatives in their own or nearby country-markets, and seeking to participate in project groups within the MNC that address issues such as entry into emerging markets or regional integration.

- They are prepared to take the risk of investing in areas such as training, advertising and promotion, and information systems in order to grow the MNC's business.

- In most cases, the other product lines carried by these distributors were complementary rather than directly competitive (i.e., their market fit is not strong).

Given the preference of MNCs for control over their own international marketing operations, these policies cannot guarantee a long-term role to even the most effective national distributor. What they can do, however, is increase the value of the distributor to the MNC in the course of their relationship and thus improve the price paid by the MNC to distributors to buy back their sales and distribution business.

The future may not be all bleak, however. There are some trends that suggest that MNCs may come full circle and start looking for effective local independent distribution partners. Many more experienced MNCs are establishing or strengthening regional management in more mature regions in which they have been active for some years. In the European Union (EU), for example, MNCs typically have national subsidiaries, each with its own sales force and management infrastructure. Given market homogenization within the EU, however, it makes sense to move towards a structure in which strategic marketing responsibility is shifted to the regional level, rendering redundant the strategic marketing capability in which they had invested in each individual country-market. In general, marketing responsibility is being shifted to the regional level and structured around product groups or market sectors. Within the general context of the globalization of markets, there are two major motivations for such moves. First, the dense network of directly owned national distributors that has grown up in the region is now thought to be inefficient in the duplication of managerial resource at country level and in the missed opportunities for economies in areas such as information systems and promotional expenditure. Second, regionalization is intended to enable greater strategic control over the business at the corporate level. This would counter pressure for autonomy felt from country management in areas such as cherry-picking from the product range, and it would also counter a reluctance to invest in innovations, such as new products, until they had been proven in other markets. Interestingly, this need for greater control echoed some of the reasons for the earlier switch from independent to direct distribution (i.e., the switch had not proved wholly remedial). In other words, there were signs that the vendor-distributor imbalance can continue beyond the distributor crisis and the switch to direct distribution and that in many cases earlier underinvestment had been corrected only by overinvestment.

In these more mature regions, there is a much greater corporate emphasis on consolidation and efficiency, and less emphasis on the developmental objectives characteristic of earlier phases of internationalization, particularly the trade-off between commitment and control. Thus, the distribution strategy decision becomes more like that in a single home market context. Because the regionalization of marketing control is an emergent phenomenon, the effect on national distributors is unclear, but it seems probable that in some cases the clarification of the role of national distributors as implementers of marketing strategy may in some cases make an indirect channel more attractive. Their role may well fall within a mixed distribution system, with major customers, especially multinational accounts, handled directly and independent distribution employed for focused segments of national markets and/or smaller accounts.

SUMMARY

For MNCs, the way in which firms adapt their approach to foreign market development over time offers insights into the long-run implications of decisions taken at the time of market entry. It appears likely that most international corporations are growing towards a global marketing network in which strategic marketing management responsibility is placed at the supranational (regional or global) level (along with production, research, and physical distribution operations), while sales and customer service remain locally focused. However, most international distribution channels appear to evolve with strategic marketing and sales force implementation vested together in a single national operation, controlled by either an independent distributor or a subsidiary. In such cases, channel structure decisions may be remedial decisions taken to correct organizational imbalances caused by the co-location of marketing strategy and sales implementation. So, while independent distributors may be the optimal vehicles with which to enter a market, strategic control of the business is sometimes sacrificed because of the low-commitment "mindset" that prevails at this stage of internationalization. Subsequent investment in channel control, however, may in turn lead to a build-up of local marketing management and programs that later become the target for elimination as the global network develops. In other words, a pattern may result of underinvestment in marketing management and control at market entry followed by overinvestment following the acquisition of channel control, which is only finally balanced at mature phases of internationalization. The emergent support available for this argument is the tendency of more experienced international corporations to make greater efforts to exercise strategic control of their business at the point of market entry in areas such as product range, communication strategies, and pricing levels.

International experience therefore influences not only the manner in which MNCs handle their portfolio of national organizations, but also their approach to new foreign market entries. The sum effect may be for experienced MNCs to focus less on channel ownership, which results in the previously described strong shift between the bipolar options of ownership or contracting, and instead to concentrate more on balancing control of marketing strategy with efficiency in implementation, resulting in a mixed distribution network. From the basis of a clearer concept of the eventual marketing organization towards which the MNC is evolving, more explicit strategies could be developed regarding the respective role of subsidiaries and independent distributors and the type of distributor to be selected as a suitable partner.

From the perspective of a distributor seeking agencies for international vendors in its own country-market, this trend can be alarming and even threatening. In research into this issue, almost all multinationals bemoaned the lack of strategic marketing capability in distributor organizations and claimed that their companies eventually made a far better job of market development after they had invested in full control of their businesses, and many suggested that the gradual globalization of competition would lead to the disappearance of many such distributor organizations. The capabilities that make distributors attractive at the point of market entry, such as a local focus and being embedded in the specific country-market, are the very qualities that hinder the relationship with the MNC as it seeks to integrate its global distribution network. The development required of the distributor organization can, of course, be either facilitated or hindered by the MNC's approach to the relationship, but it remains true that cases where an independent distributor has managed to maintain its value to an MNC vendor over time are few and far between. In principal, there appears to be no reason why distribution cannot continue to be subcontracted to specialist organizations that reap economies of scope from serving a range of principals; such arrangements, the traditional justification for the existence of distribution intermediaries, are increasingly common in areas as diverse as management information systems and human resource management. For distributors to enjoy a continued importance in the marketing systems of major MNCs, they must be able to combine an international focus and operating competence with their local sensitivity.

6

INTERNATIONAL CUSTOMER MANAGEMENT AND THE CHALLENGE OF INTERNATIONAL PRICING

It is rarely recognized that for many companies, internationalization is a reactive process rather than the result of a deliberate strategy. In such cases, it is nearly always the same factor pushing the firm towards international operations—its customers. Whereas the debate continues over whether a "global consumer" exists, many business-to-business or industrial markets have long been internationally integrated, and the ability to service a customer on an international basis is a prerequisite for participation in the market. For example, any company supplying a major manufacturing industry, such as automobiles or computers, will have to follow its clients as it relocates its production centers to low-cost economies in regions such as Southeast Asia or Central America. Even if the sales negotiations can be conducted in the domestic market, it will still be necessary to establish a service function close to the production site.

This can have a beneficial effect on a company's growth—internationalization by major customer "pull" is considerably less risky a prospect than a more detached market assessment because the initial business is virtually guaranteed. Until recently, such international supplier-customer relationships remained mostly multidomestic in their character—that is, business was conducted almost entirely at the national level, with only occasional international coordination of local transactions and relationships. However, major changes are now under way in many industries with the emergence of "global account management" (the coordination of customer management across boundaries).[1] Global account management (GAM) usually involves supplier-customer agreements, sometimes formalized in contract form, specifying standardized terms in areas such as price, product specification, and service standards. This amounts to the globalization of the sales function, traditionally the most locally managed of all marketing activities.

Global account management may seem initially attractive to many supplier companies: it offers a clear route to internationalization and the prospect of closer partnerships and therefore increased business with major international customers. In addition, it integrates with the wider efforts being made by many companies to put customer relationship management (CRM) at the heart of their business and to build customer-centric organizations. However, recent research into this new international marketing phenomenon is starting to suggest that global supplier-customer relationships often benefit the customer at the expense of the supplier, mainly because they increase the customer's ability to exert downward pressure on prices.[2]

This occurs in the context of a number of developments in the business environment that threaten the ability of an international company to exercise pricing power. Most corporations operate initially in international markets on a cost-plus pricing basis, setting price as a fixed mark-up on the

---

1. A number of descriptive labels are given to such arrangements, such as global customer management, international customer relationship management, or strategic account management (which may or may not have an international dimension). In this book, for simplicity, "global account management" will be used for all such relationships with any international dimension.

cost at the point of export. For many companies, this policy persists over at least the medium term because their distance from the international market separates them from the close-up knowledge required to adopt a more market-led pricing policy based upon demand characteristics and competitive intensity. Ironically, just as more experienced multinationals are acquiring that knowledge (and are beginning to adopt more market-oriented pricing based on customer value), they are finding that higher levels of integration in the buying departments of their major customers are threatening their ability to price to market. An unwary supplier company entering GAM arrangements without careful thought, therefore, may find that it has entered the marketing equivalent of a pact with the devil. This chapter examines the forces behind this shift in the balance of power in both customer management and pricing, outlines the traps facing the international firm, and provides guidelines for mitigating these effects. It addresses the globalization of both sales (or customer management) and price: although these are separate issues from a conceptual standpoint, they are usually inextricably related in international marketing practice.

_____

2.   This chapter draws upon a stream of recent research that can be consulted in more detail in the following publications: (1) David J. Arnold, Julian Birkinshaw, and Omar Toulan, *Implementing Global Account Management in Multinational Corporations*, Marketing Science Institute Working Paper Report No. 00-103. Cambridge, MA: Marketing Science Institute, 2000. (2) Julian Birkinshaw, Omar Toulan, and David J. Arnold, "Global Account Management in Multinational Corporations, Theory and Evidence," *Journal of International Business Studies*, Vol. 32, No. 2 (Second Quarter, 2001): 231–248. (3) David J. Arnold, Julian Birkinshaw, and Omar Toulan, "Can Selling Be Globalized?" *California Management Review*, Vol. 44, No. 1 (Fall 2001): 8–20. Two other important publications that discuss similar issues are Das Narayandas, John Quelch, and Gordon Swart, "Prepare Your Company for Global Pricing," *Sloan Management Review*, Vol. 42, No. 1 (Fall 2000) and David B. Montgomery and George S. Yip, "The Challenge of Global Account Management," *Marketing Management*, Vol. 9, No. 4 (Winter 2000).

THE EMERGENCE OF GLOBAL CUSTOMER MANAGEMENT AND PRESSURE FOR PRICE HARMONIZATION

Demands by customers for international consistency in areas such as price or service standards are not new, as any experienced international salesperson will testify. In recent years, however, these demands have become stronger and more organized for two reasons. First, in many industries, the power of intermediaries and distributors has increased due to consolidation and internationalization. Second, the buying function in many corporations has globalized rapidly, spurred by an awareness of the clear benefits of consolidating purchase orders internationally and so reaping lower volume-related price deals. In the late 1990s, it was recognized that global account management was "the new frontier in relationship marketing," that customer demand for international management was increasing sharply, and that GAM was one of the key elements of the globalization of markets.[3] It should be noted that this realization by MNCs of the need to globalize the sales or customer management function came some considerable time after the same realization in the buying function of their major customers, many of whom already had globally integrated procurement teams. A number of major multinationals subsequently restructured their sales or customer management organizations by shifting power and responsibility away from country managers to global divisions responsible for customer groups or lines of business. Significantly, these included not only industrial marketers such as Dow, but also consumer marketing companies such as Procter & Gamble, which was

---

3. G. Yip and T. Masden, "Global Account Management: The Frontier in Relationship Marketing," *International Marketing Review*, Vol. 13, No. 3 (1996): 24–42. David B. Montgomery, George S. Yip, and Belen Villalonga, *Demand for and Use of Global Account Management*, Marketing Science Institute Working Paper Report No. 99-115, Cambridge, MA: Marketing Science Institute, 1999.

facing increased demand for international buying from its newly internationalizing retail customers.[4] For many supplier companies, these demands manifested themselves in one very clear request—customers noticed that they were paying different prices in different countries, and they wanted greater consistency. Not surprisingly, the consistent price they had in mind was the lowest price available, in whichever country that happened to prevail.

A number of developments, relevant to both customer power and international pricing, have been driving this trend:

- **Information Technology**—The development of global corporate intranets and other networks external to companies such as business-to-business exchanges has resulted in a dramatically increased transparency of global pricing information and an enhanced ability of buying managers to compare the prices they are offered almost instantly. Before this technological revolution, it took considerable effort for a buyer in one region to find out the price being paid by his or her company colleague in another region.

- **Global Procurement Initiatives**—The last ten years have seen a greatly increased focus on supply chain management, partly as a response by western companies to the invasion of Japanese companies into their markets in the 1970s and 1980s. One of the outcomes of this shift in attention has been the emergence of global buying initiatives, motivated not only by the drive for lower prices but also by a desire for uniformly high quality standards. Companies have coordinated their own buying functions and have sometimes also joined multifirm buying syndicates. As globally consolidated purchases delivered cost savings, companies have seen tangible returns on the globalization of their procurement efforts.

---

4. See "Country Managers: From Baron to Hotelier," *The Economist*, May 11, 2002.

- **Customer Focus**—The development of customer-oriented management tools, such as CRM programs, has focused most firms' attention on the fact that all customers are not equal and that a small group of customers are usually responsible for a large proportion of company profits. Ironically, this has greatly increased the customers' power over their suppliers, as the dependence of these vendors was made apparent.

- **Regional Trading Blocs**—The underlying trend in many regions is towards harmonization of prices because of regional trading arrangements, the most notable being the introduction of the euro currency in the European Union. While other blocs, such as NAFT, ASEAN, and Mercosur are less advanced in this trend, they are nevertheless facilitating greater pricing consistency through measures such as tariff reduction.

- **More Sophisticated Arbitrage Networks**—Like most other businesses, the business of parallel importing or gray marketing (the arbitrage of price differences by buying low in one country, "redistributing" the goods, and then selling at a higher price in another country) has grown considerably more sophisticated. This has reduced the ability of companies to maintain price differences in neighboring countries.

These trends generally favor end consumers because almost invariably they result in a lowering of prices. In some circumstances, this can be widely perceived to result in a general benefit to society. In the UK, for example, it was long documented that car prices were significantly higher than on the nearby mainland European continent, and even the UK government joined the chorus of voices lobbying car manufacturers to reduce the differential. In the end, however, the greatest single pressure that produced a lowering of prices was the ability of British consumers to understand this fact (via new information sources) together with a new ability to sidestep the price premium via a new group of arbitrageurs that imported cars from continental Europe to Britain (via new parallel importing networks).

Nevertheless, it is worth reminding ourselves at this point that, at a fundamental level, there is no *theoretical* argument for international price harmonization (at least, until the world becomes a single market). On the demand side, the consumers of different countries place different values on the same goods for a variety of cultural and historical reasons. A fast-food meal that is an everyday price-sensitive offering in the United States can be a premium-priced novelty in a market such as China; indeed, price variation for just this very product is the basis for *The Economist* Big Mac Index, which is designed to compare purchasing power in different countries. Economic theory and marketing practice tell us that the product should be priced at the highest point of the consumer's willingness to pay so that the full value is extracted and so that the good is consumed by those who value it most. The bottom line is therefore that different prices should prevail in different countries when consumers value the same product differently. On the supply side, the fact that economies are managed by national governments ensures that there are structural differences in costs among countries, in fields such as wage rates, in labor legislation, in taxes, in real estate costs, in the cost of complying with regulation, and so on. There is simply a different cost to doing business in different countries. The bottom line is again different costs in different countries, without even considering the costs of transporting goods from one country to another in the (usually applicable) case that production is not always local.

In summary, then, there is a fundamental conflict of interests brought about by these trends. On the one hand, as a vendor, an international company should wish to pursue price discrimination across international markets (i.e., different prices in different countries), to reflect the divergent demand and cost conditions. On the other hand, as a buyer, an international company aiming to maximize the efficiency of its global supply chain should wish to pursue uniform global prices and so obtain extra discounts from the global consolidation of orders. The balance of power in the negotiations will almost certainly determine which side prevails in this conflict. Unfortunately, a number of international companies are jumping on the global account management bandwagon without realizing the challenge that faces them.

THE CONSEQUENCES OF INTERNATIONAL CUSTOMER MANAGEMENT

Recent research into GAM in Europe and North America, looking at the issues from the vendor's perspective, found management in over half the corporations surveyed reporting that unanticipated costs outweighed the benefits and struggling to figure out how to make the system work.[5] In many cases, the major change resulting from recategorizing a customer as a global account was increasing downward pressure on prices. This is illustrated in Table 6–1, which is excerpted from survey research into companies with a mix of global and local account management arrangements.[6]

It can be seen that, on average, global accounts matched other accounts in terms of sales growth, but lagged other accounts in terms of price maintenance. Such a finding is not surprising, working from the previous logic of the relative returns to globalization available to sales and procurement. However, it must come as a surprise to some executives within the companies involved, who no doubt launched global management initiatives with the objective of increased account penetration and therefore profitability.

In addition, many vendor companies were paying increased sales commission, now that both global account teams and local sales teams were involved in sales. And top sales executives were having to accept lower standards of account management than they knew from national account

---

5.   This specific data is reported in full in the publications cited in footnote 2.
6.   David J. Arnold, Julian Birkinshaw, and Omar Toulan, "Can Selling Be Globalized?" *California Management Review*, Vol. 44, No. 1 (Fall 2001): 8–20.

TABLE 6–1   The Effect of Global Account Management on Sales Levels and Prices *(Source: Arnold, Birkinshaw, Toulan, CMR 2001)*

Focus of Customer Base	NONGLOBAL Less than 20% of national sales come from formally designated "global accounts"	MIXED 20%–49% of national sales come from formally designated "global accounts"	GLOBAL 50% or more of national sales come from formally designated "global accounts"
How fast have total sales in this country grown during the past three years? (1 = 0% per year or less, 2 = 5% per year, 3 = 10% per year, 4 = 15% per year, 5 = 20% per year, 6 = >20% per year)	4.09	4.18	4.00
How does the average price of goods sold by your subsidiary compare to three years ago? (1 = much lower, 2 = slightly lower, 3 = no change, 4 = slightly higher, 5 = much higher)	2.91	2.41	1.73*
Who is responsible for pricing decisions related to global accounts in your country? (1 = primarily country sales manager, 2 = jointly by country sales manager and global account manager, 3 = primarily by global account manager)	1.92	1.76	2.24*
To what extent are sales and support in your company done on a local basis? (1 = coordinated globally, 2 = partially globally coordinated, 3 = done locally, some central coordination, 4 = done exclusively on a local basis)	3.67	3.82	3.00*

* *statistically significant findings*

times—not one of the companies researched, for example, had developed a system for measuring account profitability on a global scale. In many interviews, global account executives confided that they thought the company had jumped into global account relationships too hastily. From the customer perspective, of course, designation as a "global account" increases expectations and therefore demands with regard to service levels from the vendor in question.

In many cases, there appears to be an economic imbalance at the heart of the arrangement. There are three general issues behind many of these problems, and these issues are the major pitfalls of rapid adoption of GAM:

- The first is the economic imbalance at the heart of the relationship. For the supplier, GAM increases the cost of serving a customer because the extra GAM activities supplement rather than replace existing national sales operations: orders are still placed and booked at the national level in order to meet reporting and accounting requirements and logistics and service obviously require the same local management and operations for implementation, even if they are managed globally. For the customer, however, a major benefit of GAM is the ability to coordinate orders internationally and thus obtain higher discounts on the grounds of higher volume. The supplier may therefore be caught in a double jeopardy of higher costs and lower prices.

- There is also an organizational imbalance, a lack of fit, or a misalignment that results from globalizing supplier-vendor relationships; put simply, the buying function of most customer organizations is more globalized and internationally coordinated than the selling function of most vendor organizations. The result is that the customer, with superior global information and sophisticated supply chain management systems, has the balance of power in negotiations.

- The third issue is "ownership of the customer." A national sales organization usually feels threatened by corporate adoption of its major customer(s) as a global account. This is problematic because the local sales force is still needed to implement any global sales agreements and is involved in booking and invoicing orders, delivery, and after-sales service. Should such a sales force feel disenfranchised by the "loss" of its customers to corporate headquarters, GAM may have a net negative influence on customer satisfaction.

These issues reflect the fundamental fact that, in many respects, the sales function is a quintessentially local activity that does not globalize well. In general, MNCs have responded to increasing globalization principally by reconfiguring "upstream" elements of the value chain, such as production, R&D, and financing (in which the benefits of scale and control are most evident). Customer management has generally remained the responsibility of local subsidiaries on the grounds that the benefits of international integration are outweighed by the benefits of responsiveness to heterogeneous customer demands. The structure of MNCs has reflected this configuration of activities by delegating responsibility for marketing and sales to the national subsidiary level. Indeed, even within the marketing function, customer management is generally regarded as the most execution-sensitive of activities, and it is therefore delegated to local territories within the country organization. In addition, the allocation of responsibility for revenue generation to the national level provides a basis for a company's measurement and control systems. Figure 6–1 shows the usual configuration of marketing activities against the trade-off between the value of international integration and the value of local responsiveness.[7]

This rationale for organization design is turned on its head by GAM structure. As is shown in Figure 6–1, GAM is intended to add the benefits of global integration to customer manage-

---

7. The trade-off between integration and responsiveness is an established concept in research into multinational corporations, and this diagram draws upon this. See C. K. Prahald and Yves Doz, *The Multinational Mission: Balancing Local Demands and Global Mission* (New York: Free Press, 1987).

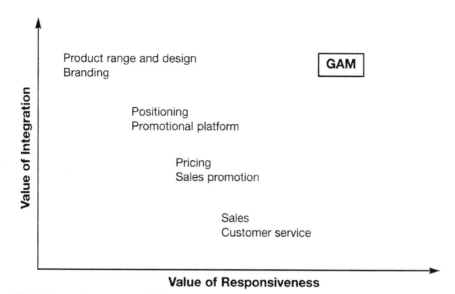

FIGURE 6–1   The Dominant Model of International Marketing Organizations

ment while retaining local responsiveness. It is ambitious at best, and it is arguably a denial of a necessary trade-off that must be made. To complicate matters further, this is not simply a transfer of responsibility for major accounts from the local to the global level—GAM units must exist alongside traditional territory-based sales units because GAM units depend upon them for execution of GAM initiatives. Therefore, although intended to increase the levels of control and consistency in customer management processes, GAM also increases the complexity and fragmentation of the vendor's international sales organization.

Two illustrative case studies from our field research highlight problems that were encountered in several companies. Consider first the experiences of Whitegoods Corp., a European manufacturing company that designated a number of global account managers in response to the centralized purchasing demands of major retail customers. These individuals negotiated the whole package with their customers—product specifications, prices, and even local installation and service agreements. Unfortunately, the Whitegoods sales organization was still managed on a country-by-country basis.

Local salespeople prioritized the higher-margin business they received through local customers. Some of the local salespeople disregarded the frame agreement altogether, with the result that global account managers found themselves "policing" the deal. And in a few countries, local sales managers were not even informed about the global accounts and only found out about them via their customers. The result was delays and disagreements on local installation and a soured relationship between national sales managers and global account managers. Prices were squeezed down as a result of the global agreement, but the projected sales volume increases did not materialize.

In a second case, it was the more manipulative behavior of a customer that sabotaged the agreement. A major customer of Computer Corporation, a U.S.-based manufacturer, had negotiated an agreement similar to Whitegoods' with a major global account in the financial services sector. The German subsidiary of that customer approached Computer Corp.'s German subsidiary for quotes on a major order for 500 workstations, required as the firm switched its European headquarters from London to Frankfurt. It wanted a price below the minimum specified in the global agreement, arguing that extra volume discounts were appropriate since the order was large, nonrecurring, and all intended for local German offices. Computer Corp.'s German subsidiary, a profit center, with much to gain from accepting the order in what was proving a difficult recessionary year in Germany, eventually succumbed to the temptation and accepted the order. It proved to be less substantive than promised, with only 100 units being purchased, a good number of which it suspected were reexported to Eastern Europe. The global agreement, meanwhile, had fallen apart as other subsidiaries of the customer received word of the lower price obtained in Germany.

These cautionary examples illustrate two of the more common problems in GAM programs. In the case of Whitegoods, the organization simply could not implement what the global account managers had agreed to. The reallocation of authority to the central global account managers had left local sales operations feeling disenfranchised, and yet they were still needed to deliver, install, and process orders. In the case of Computer Corporation, there was a failure at the strategic level to design a relationship that included partner-specific initiatives such as customized products, or joint-innovation projects. The result, perhaps the most common failing of global account management, was that the relationship reverted to a price discount play on the part of the buyer.

It is important to note that GAM units are additive rather than substitute forms of sales organization, resulting in two parallel and interdependent sales organizations. In almost all cases, GAM initiatives are executed through established national sales organizations, which are still responsible for taking and fulfilling orders and for after-sales service and local account maintenance. This not only produces doubt over who "owns" the customer, but it also means that the introduction of globalized selling results in greater fragmentation, complexity, and costs within vendor-selling organizations. In most cases, adding a GAM structure added a third dimension to the established product-geography matrix. The execution-sensitive nature of sales, which explains why this function has remained a local responsibility for so long, cannot apparently be eliminated by the introduction of global structures.

RESEARCH INTO THE PERFORMANCE OF GLOBAL ACCOUNTS

The limited research available into the performance consequences of GAM suggests that it frequently has a net negative impact upon results. As previously illustrated, in a sample of 104 global account managers from 14 companies, it was found that while sales growth was widely reported, this was often at the expense of lower prices.[8] The growth in sales could be favorably interpreted by the vendor organization, of course,

---

8. Results of this survey research are reported fully in David J. Arnold, Julian Birkinshaw, and Omar Toulan, "Can Selling be Globalized?" *California Management Review*, Vol. 44, No. 1 (Fall 2001): 8–20.

since increased account penetration is generally a primary objective of shifting accounts to GAM status. However, the decline in average unit price is of far greater consequence for the company's long-run profitability. Moreover, the same study compared these results with findings from national sales managers and found that while sales growth was similar in both types of customers, price erosion was an issue only for the global customer accounts. In other words, price erosion appears significantly worse in global accounts than in locally managed customers, suggesting that GAM does indeed provide the customer opportunities to obtain lower prices.

This study also found that the strongest predictor of the successful introduction of GAM was the establishment of *internal* information and support systems rather than any initiative related to customer interaction or sales terms. This is consistent with the previous argument about organizational misalignment, and it is also consistent with earlier research in the 1980s into national account management in the United States, which also found that internal support systems were a critical success factor in managing the complexity of large-scale multiterritory customer relationships.[9]

Similarly, we found that GAM units were more effective when their role was to coordinate dispersed actions (in local sales units) rather than when they were given full, centralized responsibility for sales decisions.

In summary, therefore, the limited evidence available suggests that there is a considerable risk that shifting to an international or a global customer model of customer management is against the interests of vendor companies. All things being equal, the structure of the relationship favors the customer at the expense of the vendor, especially in the area of price negotiation. It is therefore essential that companies internationalize their customer management efforts selectively and intelligently, ensuring that the only accounts managed internationally are

9. B. Shapiro and R. Moriarty, *Support Systems for National Account Programs: Promises Made, Promises Kept*, Marketing Science Institute Report No. 84-102, Cambridge, MA: Marketing Science Institute, 1984.

strategic (i.e., provide opportunity for partnership that creates new sources of value sufficient to cover the additional costs to serve the account). Most of the problems described so far are caused by too hasty adoption of GAM. In some cases, however, a well-managed GAM relationship has the potential to increase sales and profits from the account through strategic joint initiatives such as new product development.

GUIDELINES FOR SELECTING, DESIGNING, AND IMPLEMENTING GLOBAL ACCOUNT MANAGEMENT PROGRAMS

It is at two levels—strategy and implementation—that international companies need to make some tough decisions *before* entering global account relationships. Senior management needs to be aware of the pitfalls and to set themselves clear criteria against which relationships are examined before commitments are made.

STRATEGY—SELECTING AND DESIGNING GLOBAL ACCOUNT RELATIONSHIPS

At a strategic level, vendor companies should take a selective approach to the introduction of global account structures. It is better to start from the skeptical viewpoint that, for vendors, such relationships are inherently dangerous. In selecting the right customers to designate as global accounts, the two most important criteria are the balance of power in the relationship and the potential for strategic synergies.

ASSESS THE BALANCE OF POWER

The shark lurking in the waters of global account management is the bargaining power logic of centralized purchasing. A professional buyer looking for standard worldwide pricing is, of course, looking for the lowest price to be applied everywhere. Beyond this, a customer consolidating purchases from several countries will, reasonably, expect volume discounts against previously prevailing prices. The fact is that, in most companies, the purchasing function is considerably more globally coordinated than the sales function because it shows greater return to scale than the more execution-sensitive function of managing customer relationships. It is therefore not surprising that so many global account relationships favor the customer at the expense of the vendor.

The key determinant of the balance of power in global account negotiations is the degree of internationalization of the two partners. In many cases, for example, companies simply do not have the systems to calculate worldwide sales to a given customer: in some countries, sales go through distributors and cannot be identified by the end customer; in others, sales to an affiliate or a partner or a subsidiary of a customer are not tracked as part of the same account. If the customer is more globally coordinated than the vendor, pressure for price cuts will soon surface as a "price squeeze" (see Figure 6–2). For example, one company's advertising agency had managed to identify all advertising expenditures worldwide with the titles and channels belonging to one of the largest global media groups. The fragmentation typical of these media groups meant that they were surprised by the information and were unable to resist the demand for lower prices on the basis of global volume.

Problems can also arise from demands servicing agreements in countries where the vendor does not have a presence. One U.S.-based chemical company, for example, was surprised to receive a call demanding service from a global account at its plant in Indonesia. The vendor had no sales or service organization in that country, nor did the regional manager realize that the customer was using products there—they were sold to the Singapore buying office and then shipped on to the factory in Indonesia. Rather than antagonize the customer, this vendor flew someone out from a neighboring country; but it was an expensive solution to a problem that probably should have been foreseen.

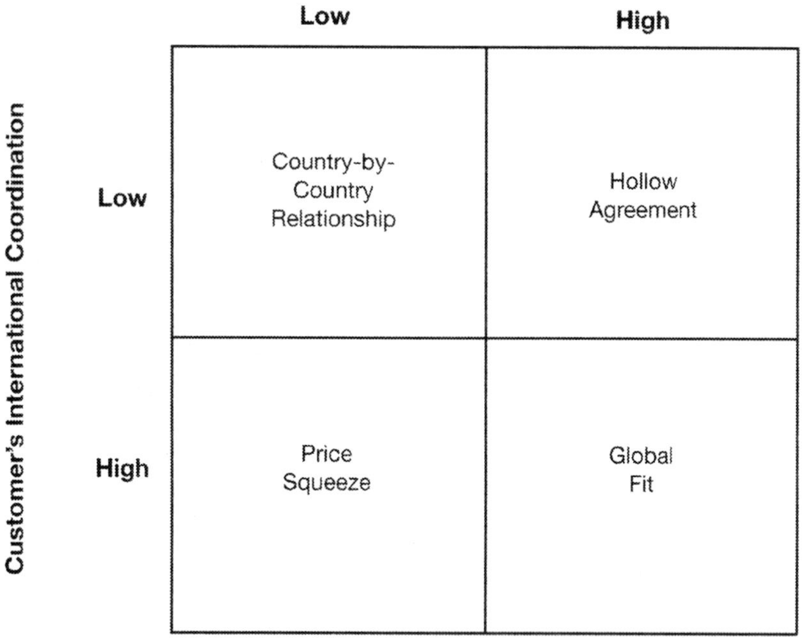

	Low	High
Low	Country-by-Country Relationship	Hollow Agreement
High	Price Squeeze	Global Fit

Customer's International Coordination (vertical axis label)

FIGURE 6–2   Vendor's International Coordination

If the vendor is more coordinated than the customer, the prospect of a global account relationship might look more attractive, but experience indicates that this imbalance will imperil the partnership in different ways, resulting in a "hollow agreement." The customer's corporate procurement executives will negotiate a global agreement even though the company is not globalized enough to make local procurement executives comply with the agreement. The resulting agreement will exist only in name, and the standardized products and services agreed upon are unlikely to take hold in the customer organization. Local buyers, without any incentive to switch suppliers, will continue to use their own local sources; some will see this as a turf issue, resenting the imposition of terms agreed by corporate executives. The customer, in other words, cannot deliver. Meanwhile, of course, the cost of serving the account has increased because of the addition of the global account organization.

In contrast, when the two sides are well matched in their internationalization, a global account relationship can work very well. Consider the case of Ericsson's relationship with Cable and Wireless. Both companies have long-established global operations. Cable and Wireless views Ericsson as its most important supplier of telecommunications equipment. In return, Ericsson rates Cable and Wireless as one of its top ten customers worldwide. Ericsson has put in place a large global account team dedicated to working with Cable and Wireless around the world as Ericsson bids for new licenses and installs leading-edge equipment. While the global account relationship exists primarily at the headquarters level in London, there are also local relationships between Ericsson and Cable and Wireless operations in a further 20 countries around the world.

ASSESS THE CUSTOMER AS A STRATEGIC PARTNER, NOT JUST A SALES ACCOUNT

Almost all the more successful global account relationships are those that are initiated by the vendor for strategic reasons. The vendor's motivation for doing so, of course, is to increase its share of the customer's business, either through guaranteed minimum levels of business or account penetration in country-markets where the share of the customer's business has been low because of local factors. But this objective only proves achievable if there is a strategic logic behind the partnership, such as the development of innovative and/or customized offerings that benefit both parties. 3M, for example, actively targets key customers in the electronics sector as partners in its product development initiatives—the targeted customers not only pass the business volume criterion, but they are judged to have resources or competencies from which 3M will benefit in the product development process. In return, the customer benefits from involvement in a relevant R&D project that will deliver customized (and in some cases exclusive) new products. Another example is Electrolux's commercial refrigeration business, which has strategic partnering relationships with Shell and other big oil companies on a global basis. For Shell, an important part of its global strategy is a common Retail Visual Identity (RVI), which means that the gas station forecourt and shop look the same wherever you go.

Electrolux is working on a range of large commercial refrigerators that fit Shell's RVI—and that push the former's product development further at the same time.

The reason to push for a strategic relationship is clear—if the relationship has no rationale other than sales "deals" on existing products and services, the negotiations will focus on price, and the globalization of the relationship will result in pressure for volume discounts. The broadening of the relationship to include strategic development projects, such as new product development or customized service agreements, is the only way to make global accounts pay for the vendor. There are three criteria for the assessment of the strategic potential of customers as global partners. If an account fails to meet any of these standards, a shift to GAM status is likely to damage performance.

Strategic Importance. There are two critical measures of importance. The first, familiar to all experienced sales executives, is the share of business accounted for by the relationship: a suitable heuristic might be whether the vendor is awarded at least half of the customer's purchases in this category. If a customer buys less than half of its supplies from a vendor and still asks to be a global account, it is likely to be a price squeeze that it has in mind. Second, is the customer a lead user of the vendor's products? This is the principal criterion 3M uses in targeting global accounts. 3M wants to be in a closer learning relationship with its lead users, even if the sales volumes do not make this customer the largest account in the sector.

Marketing and Sales Strategy. Global account relationships cannot work unless both partners are committed to global marketing. While this may seem a statement of the obvious, experience indicates that in many cases there is a serious mismatch between vendor and customer on the extent to which global consistency is part of the marketing strategy. For example, British Telecom has built a series of alliances and joint ventures around Europe in order to offer "one-stop shopping" to its international business customers. However, the reality of managing a portfolio of alliances, each with its own local partners, is that the company's approach varies from country to country. As a result, British Telecom cannot yet offer the standardized solutions that its business customers would like.

To be clear, global account management does not require that everything is centralized, but it is important that there is a compelling demand for a consistent worldwide platform for the agreement. The extent to which the customer's local marketing units are free to adapt marketing mix elements, especially products, is a good predictor of their attachment to localized purchasing.

Top Executive Support. It is vital that the account relationship operates at a senior level in both vendor and customer organizations because the relationship shifts from price negotiations to strategic issues as contacts move up through the hierarchy. Typical threshold points, at which the relationship can be said to be strategic in nature and command legitimacy, are the vice-president of supply chain management on the customer side and the vice-president of sales or marketing on the vendor side. For example, a manager in Agilent was frustrated that one of its largest accounts was being managed in what he termed a "transactional" way. He was pushing to make it a strategic account, but he acknowledged that the existing account manager—a great sales manager but not a strategic thinker—was the wrong person to take it to that level. What this account needed, and what the most successful cases have in place, is ownership at a senior level. Global account *executives* are assigned as mentors to the global account *managers*, and both groups can get together with their counterparts in the customer organization to explore opportunities for long-term collaboration.

IMPLEMENTATION—PUTTING THE RIGHT SYSTEMS AND PEOPLE IN PLACE

Customer management, or sales, has traditionally been a local responsibility (even in the largest multinationals) because it was regarded as execution sensitive and not susceptible to the economies of scale and control that have motivated globalization in other functions of the business. Global account management, in effect, turns this rationale upside down, resulting in significant tension over who "owns" the customer. In fact, research shows that the major problem encountered in new GAM structures is the conflict between the newly instituted international customer management organization, usually a corporate unit with global responsibility, and the management of a national subsidiary. Country managers are generally measured on sales revenues, and the removal of responsibility for a major customer is therefore a tangible loss. In some cases, country managers are compensated for sales to the global account originating in their country even if they play no part in the sale. The global account team also needs compensating, of course, and so in many cases the vendor organization resigns itself to double-counting orders for the purpose of compensation.

The situation is made more complex by the fact that country management involvement is still necessary in managing such a customer. Delivery and after-sales service has to be managed locally. In addition, managers assigned to the global account team are often located in the field, not in corporate units, because their location is determined by the customer organization rather than by their own. For the purposes of much day-to-day management, such as expense management, office services, and human resource issues, they are regarded as part of the national subsidiary organization.

There is no silver bullet for tackling these tensions. Managing the tension requires building up the necessary capabilities in the global sales organization and the supporting systems and structures. Here are five guidelines based on an identification of some of the key challenges encountered in field research:

CLARIFY THE ROLE OF THE GLOBAL ACCOUNT MANAGEMENT TEAM

In many companies, global account management starts out as an exercise in internal coordination—as a way of making salespeople in different parts of the company aware of what each other is doing. If the global account management program is worth establishing, however, it needs teeth, and that means moving beyond horizontal information exchange to a global line of reporting as well as a local one. For example, in

Hewlett-Packard's (HP) global account program, the Nortel Networks account manager reports to his sales manager in Canada (Nortel's home country) *and* to HP's vice president of global accounts in Palo Alto, California. The value of this matrix-like arrangement is that when conflicts arise (for example, over whether he should spend time developing the Nortel business in Europe), the global account manager has someone back in HQ to help make his case. While there need be no hard rules about when the global consideration takes precedence over local sales objectives, what should be avoided at all costs is the situation where the global account managers (in name) are simply slotted in to the country-based sales organization.

MAKE INCENTIVE STRUCTURES REALISTIC

Global account management organizations sit alongside preexisting national sales organizations rather than replacing them, and both units have a vital role in managing the account. Sales orders will still be booked through the local sales force, for example, and delivery and service are still a local job. So, who should get the sales commission when a global account places an order? This is one of the thorniest problems facing vendors. In almost all cases, it appears that vendor companies simply have to resign themselves to paying the commission twice: a payment to the global account managers based on global sales and a local payment for each order taken. This expensive solution is tolerable only if the global account program results in increased business with the customer (i.e., if the strategy is right). The lesson is clear—even if the decisions are split between global and local units, the incentive structure must be replicated at both levels as if it were a purely local responsibility.

PICK THE RIGHT GLOBAL ACCOUNT MANAGERS: NOT JUST SUPERSALESMEN

Most global account managers are recruited from the sales organization—from positions such as regional sales manager or national sales manager in small countries. This approach is misguided because a global account is very different from a portfolio of regional or national accounts. Although many regional account managers *do* make good global account managers, they have to learn some new skills to make the transition, such as understanding internal coordination, taking a long-term perspective, nurturing the account rather than milking it, and so on. Some companies take a quite different approach by appointing executives with senior line-management experience as global account managers. These individuals have all the necessary skills, and, in addition, they give the global account program its much-needed visibility.

Create a Strong Support Network. Global account management can be a lonely job, since it is by definition a networking role without a "home base." To make the role viable, therefore, global account managers need a strong support network. They need mentors back at the head office, they need information systems and communication materials to broadcast their activities, and they need regular meetings with each other at which they can compare notes and swap war stories. As previously noted, the strength of the internal support system has been found to be the single best predictor of a successful global account. Consider the case of Ericsson's enterprise networks business, which sells PBXs and office services to multinational customers. The global account managers are based in the home countries of their customers, but at headquarters in Stockholm, there is an extensive set of support activities—an order desk, marketing and customer relations, corporate network management, special project support, and internal network building. These are services that would be too expensive to spread all over the world. But perhaps more importantly, they provide the visibility and political legitimacy that the global account managers need to get their work done.

Make Sure the Customer Relationship Operates at More than One Level. As well as needing senior executive involvement, a global vendor needs to establish relationships underneath the global account manager if the commitments are to be executed effectively. Consider the comments of one local sales manager on the efforts of his global account manager: "He negotiated a frame agreement with the customer, but then he did not follow through. I only found out about the agreement when I got a call from the customer. I was made to look like an idiot, because I didn't know what he was talking about."

The most common solution to these organizational challenges is to design a GAM organization structure that mirrors the customer's organization from the global account executive right down to the local field and support team, but the reality is that except for the largest accounts (with their own dedicated people), the GAM team is composed of personnel who are "twin-hatting" (filling the GAM role as well as their position within their existing country-based sales organization). A popular way of solving the problem is to create two organizations within any country: a global customer unit that reports to the corporate locus of responsibility for that client and the territorially defined national sales organization. This is not unlike the split between national accounts and sales districts or between direct and "distribution" business.

REACTING TO INTERNATIONAL PRICING PRESSURE

However carefully international companies may manage their customer management, the environmental pressures for price harmonization, described earlier in this chapter, will continue to challenge the power to price to maximum value in all country-markets. It should be recognized that the efforts of companies to internationalize their marketing has contributed to this pressure—by offering the same products and brands in different countries, international marketers create opportunities for arbitrage. For a company seeking to offer the same products or brands in different markets, price pressure is almost inevitable either from direct customer negotiating pressure (especially for industrial or business-to-business companies) or the threat of parallel importing arbitrageurs (especially for consumer marketing companies). Even though a company should start from the assumption that different prices should prevail in different markets, and as a default option should always seek price customization, it may have to react in certain situations by compromising on price. In such situations, a key concept is that of a *price corridor*, which sets limits on the price differential between two markets.

An example is provided by the challenges facing a division of Procter & Gamble's paper business in Russia.[10] P&G had entered the former communist markets of Eastern Europe by establishing subsidiaries in each country-market and giving each profit-and-loss responsibility and a high degree of autonomy in marketing, including pricing policy. Over time, the price differentials for the product line marketed under the Always brand grew wider and wider: in Russia, highly educated and engineering-oriented consumers placed a high value on the product's superior performance and paid a premium for these functional benefits; in more price-sensitive Poland, Always faced intense price competition from cheaper local brands and had to lower its price to compete. By 1998, the price differential between the two countries was so great that entrepreneurs began buying truckloads of Always products in Poland and diverting the goods to Russia where they were resold at the higher Russian prices in street markets, which represented 50 percent of Russian retail sales in the category. The impact on the Russian business was dramatic, with Always shipments declining by 40 percent in two months. Note that P&G Poland, as a profit center judged only on its local sales performance, had incentives to accept these large orders, even if it suspected that they would be passed on to other distributors for diversion to Russia. P&G was also constrained by its policy of offering the same branded products internationally, since this eliminated one solution to the problem, offering modified versions of the product in the two markets. In the end, the only feasible solution was for P&G to take a decision at the regional level to narrow the price differential, aiming at a "corridor" that was designed to remove the incentives for the parallel importers

---

10. David J. Arnold, "Procter & Gamble: Always Russia," Harvard Business School case study 599-050, Boston: Harvard Business School Publishing, 2000.

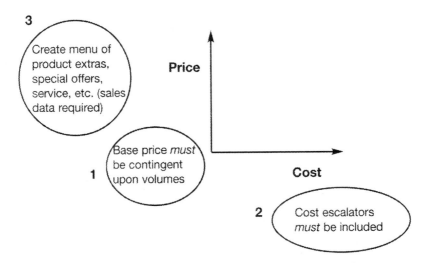

FIGURE 6–3   A Framework for Designing an International Price Agreement

(i.e., the differential was equal to or less than the costs of the diversion operation). This, of course, is a compromise, because some profit margin is sacrificed by price reduction in Russia and some sales are sacrificed by price increases in Poland. But in the interests of optimizing the performance of the international marketing program, based upon global brands, it is a rational long-term move.

In business-to-business markets, in which "global account" customers can exert direct pressure for consistent low prices, a corridor may not be sustainable; major customers may press for a specific, internationally applicable price, and they may be important enough to the supplier for refusal to be out of the question. In such cases, vendors should stick to a policy of using this agreed low price as the "base price," offering every opportunity for local variation on both the cost and demand side. Figure 6–3 outlines a three-step process for designing such a pricing policy.

Firstly, if a base price has to be conceded, it should be clearly specified that the base price is contingent upon a certain level of orders (i.e., the base price reflects a volume discount). In operational terms, this means that orders should be booked at a slightly higher price, with rebates offered retrospectively on the basis of volume. (This will avoid the generic problem described in the example of Computer Corporation earlier in this chapter.) Second, cost escalators must be included in the agreement. *Cost escalators,* a vital concept in international pricing, describes those structural differences in the costs of serving different country-markets, such as tax and labor rates, tariffs, transport, real estate, and regulatory reporting. In practice, this means that the base price will be adjusted by a country-specific charge reflecting the costs of serving the customer in that country. Although the customer might resist this concept in early negotiations, it reflects only a fact of business that the client company itself experiences, so it should be accepted as reasonable so long as there is no suspicion that the vendor is using this to cloak extra margin. It will, therefore, require some transparency on the part of the vendor in order to convince the customer that these are actual costs incurred in serving the country-market.

Finally, turning to the demand side, the vendor should do everything possible to allow buyers of the customer company at the local level to add variations to the product covered by the base price and to thus pay a slightly different price. In many cases, the local buyers of the customer company, who place the orders, will have an ambivalent attitude to the standard product/base price covered by the global agreement. This may partly reflect differences in market conditions, such as national engineering standards that influence product specification, or it may reflect personal or political motivations to establish a distinct local identity and autonomy from the corporate policy. In either case, a local buyer will wish to benefit from the global base price, but he or she will also wish to purchase extras such as product adaptations or service contracts. The vendor should therefore make available to its sales personnel worldwide a menu of possible options that local buyers can add to the standard product.

Again, this is a compromise in that it is a step back from the pure price-to-market-value approach that would be optimal. Given pressure for price harmonization from powerful customers, it is realistic, and it does attempt to introduce opportunity for price customization in local units of the global customer. Such compromises must be accepted in some circumstances, but they should not cloak the fact that price customization should remain the primary objective of international pricing policy.

SUMMARY

Global account management and the related pressure for uniform (lower) prices represent new challenges to multinational corporations. Until now, globalization has occurred mainly in "upstream" activities such as production, R&D, and financing, where benefits of scale and control are most evident. Customer management and pricing authority (or more simply, sales) have until now generally been the responsibility of local subsidiaries in order to maximize responsiveness to the heterogeneous demands of different customers and markets. Moreover, the structure of multinationals has reflected this configuration of activities: subsidiary responsibility for marketing and sales within their territory maximizes local responsiveness, and, by placing responsibility for revenue generation at the national level, it provides a basis for the company's measurement and control systems.

The trend towards global customer management undermines much of this traditional logic, and indeed it cuts against the traditional lines of organization in most large firms. Companies tend to fall into three different camps in their approach to global account management. Some like 3M are ahead of their customers, typically because they are seeking to build strategic relationships through which new technologies and products can be developed. This group essentially has nothing to fear because it is creating global accounts on its own terms. The second group is moving at the same speed as its customers. These companies are typically reacting to the initiatives of their customers, but they are quickly getting to grips with the challenge and putting programs in place to deliver on their customers' demands. For this group, the advice is to be selective. Finally, there is a group of companies that is lagging behind its customers, typically through reluctance to acknowledge the changes underway in its industry. Global account management is a real threat to these companies because they either find themselves scrambling to deliver a global account program for which they are ill-equipped or they can find themselves losing business to better-organized competitors. For this group, the need to get to grips with the globalization of the customer interface is of paramount importance. A few critical issues are as follows:

- Remember that price customization (i.e., different prices to suit the conditions of different markets or customers) should remain the primary objective of pricing policy.
- Consolidate account records so that information on global sales at the customer level is readily available. In price negotiations, information is power, and vendors without this information will find it hard to resist the demands of globally coordinated buying functions for extra discounts.
- If under pressure, establish price corridors or multipart pricing menus, including cost escalators and a menu of locally available enhancements to the standard product.
- Aim for central coordination of customer management and pricing, avoid central control, and allow for local initiative in meeting the demands of local buyers.

7 THE ORGANIZATIONAL CHALLENGE OF INTERNATIONAL MARKETING

As has been argued throughout this book, the central tension in international marketing is between the desire of international companies for consistency and simplicity on the one hand, and the complexity and heterogeneity of markets on the other. While markets are fragmenting, companies are consolidating. In managerial terms, this is the challenge of attempting to capture simultaneously the benefits of scale (mostly in terms of operations and management systems) and the benefits of local responsiveness (in terms of customized offerings to different sectors of the market). This is at heart an organizational challenge—after all, it is relatively easy for an organization to operate at one extreme of this trade-off, either sacrificing market responsiveness in pursuit of scale or sacrificing efficiency in favor of closeness to a variable market. In international situations, both factors are magnified. The potential scale available to a global corporation is what the antiglobalization movement identifies as the source of power of multinationals. However, from a corporate perspective, the added complexity of operating across multiple national regulatory regimes and market segments is even more challenging.

This tension between the corporate power of integration and the market value of responsiveness is often manifested in organizational terms. Consider a number of typical issues: should a company standardize its brand names across a number of countries and switch from the different local brands it originally acquired when it entered the market? Should the company establish price corridors that constrain the local discretion in pricing to within defined boundaries? Should customer management be adapted to include a global account team, and should product listings and service standards be agreed internationally for customers? In all these cases, it is almost certain that the managers from the national unit will favor the option that provides for the greatest local variation and management responsibility, and corporate managers will favor the supranational approach and place a high value on international consistency. Indeed, any executives or consultants experienced in international marketing management will probably be able to predict the positions taken by different players if they know their location on the organization chart. Because of this, it is often concluded that the issue has become "politicized," meaning that the debate is as much about the power balance between the different organizational units as about the substantive issue at stake. While not denying the importance of such political issues, it should also be pointed out that each party is behaving rationally according to its objectives within the organization. In other words, the organizational design is capturing the underlying forces of integration and responsiveness and placing them in opposition. It is inevitable that a company operating in international markets will have to wrestle with this tension. The challenge it faces, above all, is to design an organization that can leverage the diversity of its environment to achieve greater knowledge and scale than local, focused competitors.

This chapter begins by examining how organization structures evolve as a company internationalizes.

THE EVOLUTION OF INTERNATIONAL MARKETING ORGANIZATION STRUCTURES

The obvious way in which organizations adapt to increasing participation in international markets is through restructuring. The seminal framework on the evolution of multinational corporations is the stage model of Stopford and Wells from 1972.[1] This describes the influence over time on the organization structure of the level of foreign sales as a proportion of total corporate revenues and the diversity of product in international markets.

Its starting point is the existence of a single international division that is responsible for all sales outside the home market. This consolidation of international operations into a single division is common after fragmented foreign activities have been undertaken by a number of the core divisions of the company, and it is common before international sales represent a significant proportion of corporate revenues. From here, the international business can evolve in one of two ways. Either it expands its international sales without significant innovation in its product line (i.e., international revenues are mostly incremental sales of products available in the domestic market), in which case area divisions are established as international business grows, or it grows by offering a diversified product range in international markets, in which case a structure based on product divisions is often established.

Most companies evolve through the more southerly route in Figure 7–1, growing international sales mostly through developing foreign revenues of existing product lines. Thus, the most common form of international organization is that of area divisions, with a typical structure being divisions for

---

1.   John M. Stopford and Louis T. Wells, *Managing the Multinational Enterprise: Organization of the Firm and Ownership of the Subsidiary* (New York: Basic Books, 1972).

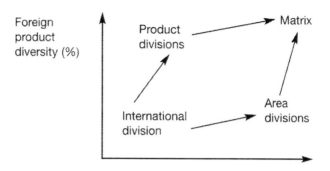

FIGURE 7–1 The Evolution of International Organizations *(Source: Stopford and Wells)*

North America, Latin America, EMEA (Europe, Middle East, and Africa) and Asia-Pacific. This is arguably the more "natural" form of international organization because markets and economies remain nationally regulated and internationalization therefore requires establishment of national operating units for purposes of accounting, reporting, and other formal functions. It is particularly suited to international businesses that remain relatively homogenous in terms of product lines, and it also usually targets customer segments as the company enters new markets. The benefits include closeness to the market (and, in particular, to distribution). An area division structure is therefore well suited to high-distribution intensity businesses, such as consumer marketing companies. The major disadvantage is that this structure is resource intensive because each country will have all the elements of a fully fledged company. This in turn leads to the strengthening of a local perspective in the company, which can lead to the development of local fiefdoms and to much tension between the local unit and the global company. The main source of global-local tension in multinationals undoubtedly springs from the existence of strong national operating units.

Alternatively, a firm may grow by offering different products in international markets, and its "foreign product diversity" increases in pace with its internationalization. In such instances, product divisions are established, which cut across geographically defined units such as national subsidiaries. Such a pattern might be common in culturally bound product categories, such as food, in which local taste dictates product adaptation, or in industrial markets such as electrical equipment, in which local technical and engineering standards require different product specifications. Most commonly, it is seen in technology-oriented companies or business-to-business firms because they frequently have a portfolio of quite distinct product lines, which often have customer profiles and distribution channels that vary more among product lines than among countries. Thus, Whirlpool has global business units for its air conditioner, commercial laundry, and consumer white goods product ranges. The advantages of these structures are firstly, the necessary scale to support product development and/or production and secondly, the integration required to deal with industrial suppliers, customers, alliance partners, or distributors that are frequently international themselves. This emphasis on scale and integration produces, unsurprisingly, the major disadvantage of such a structure—it too easily leads to remoteness from the market and an inability to adapt to differences in demand in different markets. This will of course result in a company leaving money on the table in the form of underpenetration in individual markets. In addition, it can lead to duplication of corporate resources: given the fact that the company will still require national subsidiaries for reporting and regulatory purposes, a company might have multiple product division infrastructures in any one country.

There are two main drivers of these variations:

- The major source of differentiation within a company's business becomes the major axis around which the organization is structured. Thus, companies with greater product variety favor product divisions, while companies with similar product lines across diverse country-markets favor area divisions. The underlying principle is that the organization structure is designed to contain complexity and thus to enable managers to maintain greater focus on their business objectives.

■ Each of the two major organization forms (organizing around product lines or geographical markets) pushes a company further towards one side of the trade-off between integration and responsiveness, the principal dynamic of international business. Thus, it becomes harder for a company structured around product divisions to be market driven and for a geographically structured company to achieve the benefits of scale and integration. This may suit a company operating in a market that is clearly either globally integrated or entirely local in its character. But for the majority of businesses that grow to operate with complex market and product portfolios, these solutions do little to equip a company to address the organizational challenge because they are single-dimensional solutions to a multidimensional environment.

A logical solution to this complexity facing international organizations is the matrix structure, as shown in Figure 7–1. A matrix organization structure consists of multiple reporting lines—most commonly in international marketing situations, the coexistence of the product and area divisions previously discussed. The disadvantage is obviously the complexity of the structure, which can produce two types of negative consequences. First, the lack of a single clear reporting line can blunt the incentives of local operating units and reduce the ability of senior management to manage corporate performance through a clear line of sight to profit centers with responsibility and accountability. Second, the complexity can also produce a diffusion of the power structure within the company and thus encourage turf battles between apparently equal players such as product groups and area divisions, slowing decision processes and distracting management from the overall corporate objectives.

The logic of the matrix structure as an appropriate response to increasing international complexity prompted several multinational firms to adopt this organizational form in the mid-to-late 1990s, even though the matrix structure had previously become rather discredited on the grounds that it resulted in bureaucracy and confusion. The main perceived failing of matrix structures had always been the blurring of reporting lines, so that an individual executive or business unit might have two bosses: as companies evolved their control systems to emphasize accountability and rewarded this through means such as share options and large performance bonuses, many matrix structures were dismantled. As increasing corporate globalization produced a resurgence in these complex structures, a review by one noted authority on organizational structure, John Hunt, was therefore tellingly entitled "Is Matrix Management a Recipe for Chaos?"[2] Notable examples of reorganization into matrix structures are Gillette (which organized into area divisions and product divisions, such as grooming products and stationery) and Ericsson (which designed a matrix of area divisions and segment-related divisions such as network operators, retail consumers, and corporate customers). While acknowledging the potential of matrix structures to adapt to dynamic and complex market environments, Hunt also emphasizes that companies need to retain some clear boundaries of authority alongside the ambiguity that the matrix would release.

Procter & Gamble has also recently been wresting with its matrix structure in recent years, amid much publicity. Its previous matrix was structured around country-based units with profit and loss responsibility and global product units—since the local units had profit responsibility, they had ultimate authority, and the product units had no option but to enter long negotiations to get their product initiatives adopted by the local operating units. The new strategy introduced from 1999, known as "Organization 2005," attempted to reduce this complexity by structuring the business around eight product-based "global business units" (GBUs), such as Beauty Care or Paper Products. These GBUs were designed to have profit responsibility, so they had primacy over national operating units in terms of management decision making. From the out-

---

2. John Hunt, "Is Matrix Management a Recipe for Chaos?" *Financial Times*, January 12, 1998.

set, however, certain geographical units were regarded as so distinctive in their needs that they existed outside the GBUs—an example was the Central and Eastern Europe Division covering a number of emerging markets, including Russia. More recently, it appears that P&G has made further local variations from the global consistency and control of the GBUs and the global branding strategies that flowed from them.

As these examples illustrate, the quest for the optimal structure seems to be never ending, with pendulum swings from centralization to decentralization. While the matrix structure mirrors the multidimensional nature of the environment in which international companies operate, it undermines the clear lines of responsibility and accountability that most companies seek, and so it is rarely stable in its pure form (in which the multiple reporting structures exist as equals). This is the international marketing challenge in organizational form. The problem with a matrix structure is that it remains a structural answer to process problems. In other words, imposing a matrix structure does not mean that the organization works as a matrix. The processes of international marketing, summed up in the deceptively simple phrase "think globally, act locally" are the ways in which a company manages the tension between integration and responsiveness, and so they should be the basis for organization design. A network organization appears to be the solution best suited to the organizational challenge for a firm operating in many and varied international markets. Before describing this model, it is important to understand the shortcomings of the division or area structures and identify the key processes that an organization needs to manage in international markets.

THE ORGANIZATIONAL PROBLEM— HORIZONTAL AND VERTICAL PROCESSES

The division-based international organization is based on the premise that the complexity characteristic of a large multinational corporation can best be managed by dividing it up into controllable units and by plotting clear reporting lines of responsibility among those units. This inevitably means a hierarchy of layers of management. While this does indeed improve management from a local perspective, it can actually hinder the pursuit of the company's higher goals of being simultaneously a large organization and a responsive or market-driven one. In other words, there is no net reduction in complexity, since any improvement in local managerial clarity is exceeded by the increased complexity of the multinational structure.

The problem is illustrated in Figure 7–2, which shows a portion of a typical division-based multinational organization structure. The complexity of this structure is immediately apparent, although in fact the organization could be even more complex if, for example, product divisions existed alongside area or regional divisions or if there were a global manufacturing organization centered on a limited number of factories for which some countries were responsible.

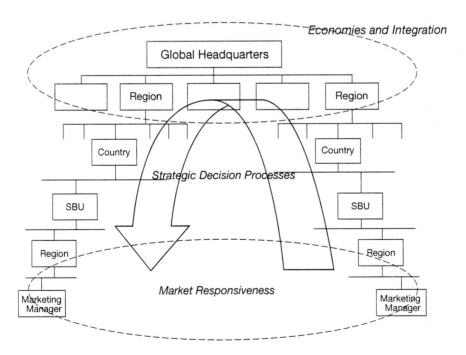

FIGURE 7–2   The Challenge of Divisional International Organizations

The first major problem with this structure is that it fails to reconcile the twin aims of scale and responsiveness. As is clear from the diagram, these are (in organizational terms) horizontal processes (i.e., they take place among a number of units that are at the same level in the organization). Scale economies and integration are necessarily best managed at the top of the organization, and they will be derived from cross-management of major units of the organization. Market responsiveness is obviously maximized at the "bottom" of the organization, in those units closest to the customer. And yet this organization structure is essentially vertical in that information and responsibility flows up through the levels rather than across among units on the same level.

The second major problem is that this type of organization tends to be slow in making decisions and remote from the marketplace from which it derives its revenue. The slowness is a function of the number of layers between the market interface (at which point market information and research is generated) and the higher authorities in the corporation. This is true of all large hierarchical organizations, but it is greatly exacerbated in multinationals because the cultural and administrative gap among national units is necessarily greater. The remoteness from the market is similarly a consequence of this multilayered nature—almost by definition, those at the global headquarters are removed from the market in a way that national managers cannot be.

The third major problem is the fact that strategic decision processes go up and down (rather than across) levels. There are good reasons for this, of course—the senior management of a company will wish to have "line of sight" through to individual market-based units in order to fine-tune their performance measurement, accountability, and reward systems within the organization and so maximize profit at the local level. However, this does mean that the horizontal processes of integration and responsiveness are minimized. At the market level, for example, there is no mechanism or incentive facilitating the exchange of market information or learning from one national unit to another. Yet, it is widely recognized that one of the advantages of international firms should be this ability to transfer learning from one market to another, both to improve performance through transfer of best practice and to obtain the maximum leverage in introducing innovations to the market.

The underlying tension in international marketing organizations is between the corporate center and the local operating unit, which of course replicates the tension between the benefits of scale and integration and those of local autonomy and responsiveness. As the following case examples demonstrate, an organization needs to be flexible enough to integrate when necessary and needs to encourage local market-driven initiatives when necessary. In both cases, the organization needs to have a structure that permits reorientation to the shifting center of gravity.

TWO EXAMPLES OF AN INTERNATIONAL MARKETING ORGANIZATION

The consequences for international marketing of organizational issues are well illustrated by two detailed case histories of BRL Hardy, the Australian-based wine company, and Acer, the Taiwan-based computer company.[3]

In the case of BRL Hardy, the main organizational tension is between the Australian headquarters and the strong UK subsidiary—traditionally the company's largest local marketing company, it operates in the world's largest export market for Australian wine. The UK company had not only succeeded in achieving strong sales for BRL Hardy's core range of Australian wines, but it had also begun undertaking local initiatives (including the development of new brands based upon

3.   Christopher A. Bartlett, "BRL Hardy: Globalizing an Australian Wine Company," Harvard Business School case study 9-300-018. Christopher A. Bartlett, "Acer America: Development of the Aspire," Harvard Business School case study 9-399-011. Boston: Harvard Business School Publishing.

research into the UK market) and sourcing from vineyards in Chile and Italy. As it positioned the company's Australian brands further up market, the UK company also developed an entry-level Australian wine brand called Kelly's Revenge (which was aimed at a distinctive segment of the UK market) at the same time as the parent company was seeking global roll-out of its new Australian brand Banrock Station.

The tension arose because the culture of BRL Hardy allowed considerable local autonomy—quite reasonably, since wine markets show distinct international differences in consumption patterns, tastes, and distribution. Moreover, the UK subsidiary had a recent track record of success and was obviously in close touch with the dynamics of its market. In such circumstances, there seems only a weak case for insisting that the UK company devote some of its resources to launching the company's new "corporate" Australian brand rather than its own locally targeted brand.

The key failure in this case is a network failure—the UK subsidiary is acting as an effective distributor of BRL Hardy's globally marketed Australian brands, but the company's network is not leveraging the subsidiary's innovative marketing for the greater benefit of the group. To use the analogy employed in an influential paper on multinational organizational design by Julian Birkinshaw, the UK subsidiary is an island, not a peninsula.[4] The lack of international networking of effective local marketing is fuelling the subsidiary's quasi-isolationist approach, which eventually leads to resistance to marketing initiatives coming from headquarters. The company could have managed this better by doing the following:

■ Organizing a global sourcing policy and making its benefits available to all local units rather than allowing a situation to develop in which the UK subsidiary takes its own initiative in sourcing grapes from other countries. Sourcing is one area in which the whole company can

---

4. Julian M. Birkinshaw and Neil Hood, "Unleash Innovation in Foreign Subsidiaries," *Harvard Business Review* (March 2001).

benefit from global integration, given the risks in grape production (a possible scarcity of supply due to poor harvests) and foreign exchange risks. This activity should be managed from the center.

- The subsidiary's initiatives should be leveraged across the company's global network instead of merely being locally permitted, as at present, because they show a profit. The Italian brand, based upon images of Mediterranean lifestyle and close links with food, clearly has additional potential in markets beyond the United Kingdom. The corporate center should be looking at local initiatives with a view to global exploitation as well as local profit maximization.

- The subsidiary's management should be integrated into the international corporation to encourage this networking. This can be done in a number of ways: the subsidiary's senior executives could be promoted to headquarters in Australia; their remuneration could include bonuses for sales of their brands beyond the United Kingdom; or they could be designated as the lead market for certain brands that they have developed. Any or all of these changes could prevent the slide into "us and them" confrontation between a strong subsidiary and global headquarters.

By contrast, the development of Acer's multimedia Aspire personal computer illustrates a failure of integration. This is a market that is globalized, with relatively similar consumer preferences, and it requires globally integrated management because of the economies of scale in production of high-volume, short life cycle products. Like BRL Hardy, Acer was a company that emphasized local autonomy, and as a result, the U.S. subsidiary developed a winning product idea—one of the first multimedia PCs that almost flew off the shelves in its first weeks in market. However, a number of product quality problems led to a high rate of returns, an overloaded service system, and subsequent forecasting and inventory problems.

Again, it was reasonable to encourage the U.S. subsidiary to develop this innovative product—in this case, because the United States, and particularly California (where Acer America

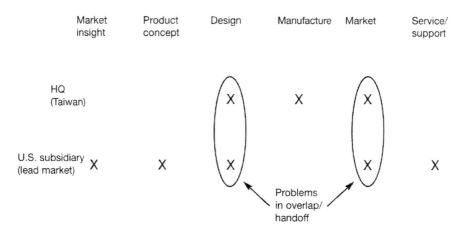

FIGURE 7–3 Acer—Managing the Handoff between Headquarters and Local Unit

was based at the time), is the lead market for PCs. The winning product concept and design would not have been developed at all in Taiwan. However, the problems arose because of a lack of integration between the marketing unit in California and the production operation in Taiwan, which had to remain consolidated because of the importance of scale economies and the complexity of production. There were inadequate processes to hand off the marketing design to the production operations.

In this case, since the initiative took place in the world's lead market, the challenge was not to integrate the local unit into the global network, but, on the contrary, to bring the global network to the support of the local unit. The company could have managed this better by doing the following:

■ Transferring production and sourcing executives from Taiwan to California at the earliest possible stage, so that the product design would incorporate the company's tested quality processes and qualified suppliers. In this way, the company could have avoided the product quality problems that eventually proved so costly.

■ Provide R&D funding to the U.S. subsidiary so that it could simultaneously continue its local operations as a profit center, and develop the new Aspire at full pace.

■ Establish a global marketing group for the new product, consisting of relevant executives from the various regional operations of the company. It should be clear that the United States is the leader of this group and retains full responsibility (with corporate support) for the development of the product.

It is clear that in both cases, vertical management processes, which inevitably lead to conflict between central and local units, hindered the company from capturing the value created by its local subsidiaries. Moreover, these vertical reporting lines also hindered even the local units from fully exploiting their ideas in the way that a local single-market company could have done. The two requisites for a company seeking to manage these processes in a way that reinforces the advantage of being international are first, horizontal communication channels that facilitate rapid and effective transfer of learning from one market to another and, second, enough centrifugal energy to allow it to shift support to a local center of gravity rather than assuming that all strategic initiatives should come from the corporate center. The network model of organization is the answer to these problems.

NETWORK ORGANIZATIONS—A TEMPLATE FOR INTERNATIONAL MARKETING

The characteristics of a network organization have been best described by Christopher A. Bartlett and Sumatra Ghoshal in their breakthrough work on multinational organization, *Managing Across Borders*,[5] a book that, although it is not concerned specifically with marketing organizations, nevertheless provides a template for helping organizations address the challenge of operating in different markets and simultaneously

---

5. Christopher A. Bartlett and Sumatra Ghoshal, *Managing Across Borders: The Transnational Solution* (Boston: Harvard Business School Press, 1989).

being responsive to each. The underlying principle is that the organization is decomposed into small units specialized enough to be responsive to local market conditions, but they are integrated into a network designed to allow frequent and multidirectional communication flows and they are flexible enough to reallocate resources to any emergent lead market or promising idea.

Bartlett and Ghoshal identify three distinguishing strengths of the integrated network. First, assets are dispersed rather than concentrated at the center. In marketing terms, this may mean that a national operating unit is the lead market for a product category. It may also mean that strategic marketing planning is conducted at the country or regional level rather than at the global center, which should improve market sensing and responsiveness. Second, some local units specialize in a particular market segment or product technology. Third, there are links of interdependence among units rather than each unit having its own links only with the center via the levels of management above it on the organization chart.

The concept of a network organization is well portrayed graphically (see Figure 7–4). A number of features characterize network structures:

- Most importantly, there is much less power at the center of a network organization than at the top of a hierarchical structure. Indeed, in operational terms, it can be said that there is no center. This means that, ideally, decisions get made in a collaborative manner rather than being handed down from above for implementation. It also overcomes the problem of the center being remote from the market.
- Units relate as equals: although different units perform different roles in the organization, they relate as equal in status and power rather than as superiors or subordinates in the line-reporting processes of a hierarchy. In many cases, therefore, a regional product division and a geographically oriented marketing unit can collaborate without one reporting to the other.

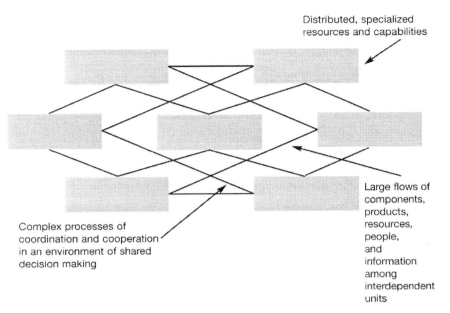

Distributed, specialized
resources and capabilities

Large flows of
components,
products,
resources,
people,
and
information
among
interdependent
units

Complex processes of
coordination and cooperation
in an environment of shared
decision making

FIGURE 7–4   The Integrated Network *(Source: Bartlett and Ghoshal, Managing Across Borders)*

- Units have multiple relationships: in contrast to the strictly defined vertical reporting lines of a hierarchy, the constituent units of a network organization relate to any other unit as necessary. This of course vastly increases the load and complexity of communication processes within the corporation.

- Units are differentiated: within a network, units of similar size and apparent function can in fact play quite different roles within the organization. For example, one national operating unit might be essentially a manufacturing organization regarded by the rest of the company as a sourcing unit and another might derive all its revenues from local sales of imported goods, but the two look identical on an organizational chart. In such a network, local units may enjoy considerable freedom to change the task they fulfill for the company in response to local opportunities and conditions.

The network model is particularly suited to marketing operations because it enables support to be reallocated as the exigencies of the market shift the center of gravity. If, for example, a competitor enters a new market and adopts penetration marketing policies in order to gain market share rapidly, a network organization can quickly draft in extra resources, managerial and product based, in order to maintain its position. In traditional hierarchical organizations, it would be the responsibility of the center to address this issue, since other units act as self-interested and relatively isolated profit centers, and the center would probably react slowly and underestimate the importance of the issue. A military analogy is insightful—in the words of a former military officer, "In war, nobody supports the center—the center supports the center of gravity, wherever that may be."[6] Since international markets are varied and changeable, the ability of a network to shift resources rapidly is of special value. The key to understanding many of the examples discussed in this chapter so far is to identify the center of gravity—this changes more rapidly and unpredictably than can be captured by a formal organization structure—or restructure.

DESIGN PRINCIPLES FOR INTERNATIONAL MARKETING ORGANIZATION

The network organizational model is of value to international marketing because it offers processes suited to the particular challenge of operating across markets. From this, it is possible to draw general principles of designing international marketing organizations.

---

6. I am indebted for this insight to one of my students, Robert Betts, a member of the Harvard Business School MBA class of 2002.

ENSURE THAT SOMEBODY HAS A GLOBAL OVERVIEW OF EACH PRODUCT LINE OR BRAND

While network structures can free a company from the rigidities of a hierarchical or division-based organization, there is also the risk that they cause a loss of the clarity and focus that exist at the top of such hierarchies. In international marketing organizations in particular, there is a strong pull from market-placed organizations. It is vital, however, that the organization retains a single locus of responsibility with a world view of the product line or brand. Otherwise, there is little chance of transferring learning from market to market, of leveraging international ideas for promotions, and of achieving marketing economies of scale in buying advertising, sales materials, or market research. The major difference in network organizations is that this global oversight need not be located in corporate headquarters, but it is vital that it is established and recognized worldwide. The obvious location for this global oversight is in the "center of gravity" of the product line or brand organization, which may or may not be the same as the corporate center or headquarters. The center of gravity can also be viewed as the lead market, in which the product competes with the other leading global competitors and deals with the world's most sophisticated customers and/or distributors, and in which product innovations first appear. Thus, for example, Ford runs its small vehicle design and marketing from Europe, the lead market for this class of automobile, but its larger sports utility vehicle unit is based in the United States.

DESIGN ACCORDING TO DECISION STRUCTURES

The real difference among international marketing organizations is frequently not evident from organization charts, which are often very similar (with boxes labeled "corporate," "region," "country," and so on). In reality, two organizations with identical structures (in these terms) might be quite different in terms of the authority given to a level within the hierarchy, such as the country marketing manager. The real difference lies in decision authority—the location of decision rights on a number of different marketing functions. An excellent example of this is described in detail in the influential paper "Customizing Global Marketing" by John A. Quelch and Edward J. Hoff, in which the decision structures of Coca-Cola and Nestlé are compared.[7] In general terms, Coca-Cola is a relatively centralized organization, while Nestlé allows local managers greater autonomy. This is explained by a number of factors, including the product range and the history of the internationalization of the companies involved. The important point is that the differences emerge from decision structures rather than from any organization chart. Thus, for example, brand names and advertising copy are both fully controlled from Coca-Cola's Atlanta headquarters, while Nestlé's country-based executives have partial autonomy over brand name and full authority over advertising copy.

It is a sound principle that organizations should be designed according to decision processes rather than power relationships. In marketing, this requires a clear mapping of the decisions that have to be made, from the more strategic level (e.g., market selection and product design) through to the tactical (e.g., net price and sales promotions). There is no generalizable "correct" configuration, since the economics and dynamics of each industry and the culture of each corporation will produce different philosophies in terms of integration and responsiveness.

ADOPT A BOTTOM-UP APPROACH TO MARKETING INNOVATION

Although many corporations establish R&D as a central function, there is a set of innovations that comes best from the

---

7. John A. Quelch and Edward J. Hoff, "Customizing Global Marketing," *Harvard Business Review* (May–June 1986).

local market-facing units. To be truly market driven, a company needs local units to be involved in new product development, new processes for customer relationship management, or new creative ideas for promotion. There are a number of examples of products that started as local innovations but eventually became international successes: *dulce de leche*, a strong-selling flavor of Häagen-Dazs ice cream, originated in the company's operations in Argentina, where this flavor of drink was a local staple, and NCR's global leadership in the manufacture of automatic teller machines (ATMs) was driven by product and operations innovations in the company's unit in Scotland, not at its U.S. headquarters.

The principle behind this is that significant innovation need not come from the corporate headquarters. Indeed, it seems more likely that market-driven innovation (as opposed to production technologies, for example) will come from local operating units because of their constant interaction with the market. Yet, in many companies, the corporate headquarters regards innovation or R&D as one of the ways in which it adds value to local operating units, which it regards as implementers and operators. In more advanced multinational corporations, by contrast, there has been an explicit recognition that the center does not have the monopoly on innovation.

INVEST HEAVILY IN HORIZONTAL COMMUNICATION CHANNELS AND INFORMATION FLOWS

It is extraordinary how often managers in the different national units of a multinational have never met each other. This is of course a function of the vertical information flows and strategic decision process that have already been described. It is essential for a multinational to leverage its wide market footprint by transferring marketing knowledge among markets. It remains true that although national operating units have superior capability in terms of operations (i.e., they know how to do business in their own country), it is the corporation that usually has superior capability in marketing its particular product range. Too often, national subsidiaries or independent national distributors are isolated units charged with making their own profit goals rather than units in a network attempting to maximize network profit instead of their own.

SMALL ORGANIZATIONS "BORN GLOBAL" INTO INTERNATIONAL MARKETS

The entrepreneurial boom of the 1990s along with the increased globalization of many markets have led a number of observers to question the previously established wisdom that internationalization was a gradual process of increasing commitment to foreign markets, as described in Chapter 5. This wisdom was stimulated by the emergence of a number of start-up companies that operated internationally almost the day of the foundation and that have become known as "born globals," a descriptive label coined by S. Tamer Cavusgil and Gary A. Knight, who described such companies as being indicative of "an emerging paradigm for international marketing."[8] This is essentially an organizational issue, since the gradualism of established models is explained by the learning process of the firm (about foreign markets) and an increasing commitment to international operations, both of which are capabilities acquired over time rather than the instant consequence of managerial decisions. So how do start-ups, with extremely limited resources and no acquired experience or learning, manage to internationalize instantly?

■ Born globals are predominantly business-to-business marketing firms. This is in line with one of the central themes

---

8. Gary A. Knight, "Emerging Paradigm for International Marketing: The Born Global Firm," Ph.D. dissertation, Department of Marketing, Michigan State University, 1996. See also Gary A. Knight and S. Tamer Cavusgil, "The Born Global Firm: A Challenge to Traditional Internationalization Theory," *Advances in International Marketing*, Vol. 8. (Greenwich, CT: JAI Press, 1996).

of this book—that businesses are globalizing faster than end-consumer markets. Any company with other businesses as its customers can therefore expect demand to be international rather than restricted to one market.

■ Born globals also frequently possess a differentiated product or technology, often patented, as the basis of their marketing strategy. This is of course likely to be true of any sample of start-up businesses. However, there is added significance in the born global group: the unique differentiated technology that it is selling is likely to diffuse rapidly across markets because of a lack of competition, and because of the international character of their customer base. These companies are often therefore operating in niche markets, in which their products are rapidly adopted by a relatively small group of specialized customers.

■ Born globals often internationalize through individual customer accounts rather than by choosing countries to enter. A major international customer who values the innovative product will want to adopt it in multiple countries.

■ Born globals cannot, as start-ups, afford to invest in dedicated national distribution channels, so they often employ indirect or hybrid forms of market participation in order to serve these major customers. These include local agents and importers, joint ventures, distribution and service consortia established by an ad hoc group of international companies, or close relationships with either major customers or other personal contacts of the entrepreneur principal. Customers can be managed in the domestic market rather than locally, leaving only a restricted range of distribution functions to be executed locally, including physical distribution, warehousing, and delivery.

■ Often, therefore, client patronage is a driving force behind the internationalization of born global firms. With limited resources and experience, start-ups rely on support from major client accounts in areas such as establishment of offices, service operations, and financing arrangements. Although such support is entirely alien to the relations the major customer usually designs with its suppliers, start-ups often regard such support as in their interest, since otherwise they would not be able to adopt the product technology across their own international operations. It is not unusual for the international customer to negotiate some degree of exclusivity of supply in return for this support, so that the two firms enter a quasi-alliance rather than conducting transactions on a pure open-market basis.

It is the niche marketing strategy, sometimes even a strategy built around one or a few individual customers, that allows small firms to be "born global." First, being born global reduces the degree of difference between the home and international market context. Rather than entering country-markets that are qualitatively different from the home market (requiring adaptation and learning beyond the resources of a small young company), a born global company addresses only those customers it knows, and it therefore internationalizes within the bounds of a single customer account. Secondly, this situation reduces the economic deterrents to market entry: focus on a well-defined niche allows a born global company to address only a few customers in any one market, and on the assumption that it serves them internationally, it can do so without significant investment in a national distribution channel, combining a local indirect presence with a global customer relationship function in the customer's home market. Thirdly, it reduces product adaptation needs, since the niche is consistent across borders.

It should be noted, however, that these characteristics are unlikely to last over the long run. Most born global companies, as is true of many start-ups, either grow or fail within a few years of foundation. As a born global company becomes larger, it will inevitably expand beyond this niche and so establish operations in international markets that seek additional local business in order to increase local market share. As this transpires, the company is likely to encounter many of the challenges typical of any internationalizing firm, and in the opportunistic, focused, rapidly changing foreign market, the company is likely to encounter many of the challenges typical of any internationalizing firm.

SERVICE ORGANIZATIONS—DIFFERENT STRUCTURES LEAD TO MORE RAPID INTERNATIONALIZATION

It is clear that market entry is less costly for a service organization than for one of its manufacturing counterparts. Interestingly, the different economic structure of service companies suggests a number of ways in which the internationalization challenge may differ for this sector. Based on the experiences of international service companies, and on some of the concepts outlined in this book, it can be hypothesized that service companies are more likely to benefit from first-mover advantage than manufacturing firms, are the enabling condition that many emerging markets need to develop, and are more likely to benefit from local product adaptation.

FIRST-MOVER ADVANTAGE AND SERVICE BUSINESSES

As was discussed in Chapter 3, first-mover advantage does not automatically accrue to the first entrant in a market, but exists only when (firstly) a scarce marketing resource is available to the entrant and (secondly) that resource can be tied up in a way that prevents it from being also available or switching to a competitive company. In general, scarce marketing resources are structural rather than attitudinal; in other words, there is less value in being the first to register in a customer's mind (because that mind is able to absorb new information as soon as it is available) than in obtaining an exclusive agreement with the only competent distributor in a country or in obtaining a government license because these assets are relatively scarce and only reproduce over time. This difference in value is because relationships are sticky, with high switching costs. Interestingly, the average service business is far more reliant on relationships than its manufacturing counterpart: very often, the relationship is what is being sold, and often the customer is involved in the delivery and/or "consumption" of the service. By contrast, finished goods enter a distribution system and can be bought and sold down the value chain in relative anonymity. Since relationships constitute a common source of first-mover advantage, it can be deduced that service companies are more likely to reap the benefits of pioneering market entry, on average, than a manufacturing firm.

SERVICE BUSINESSES AS THE ENABLERS OF THE MASS MARKET

Much of the marketing infrastructure of a country, which enables mass markets to develop, is in the service sector. This includes banking and affiliated services such as money transmission and credit assessment; advertising, promotion and design services; the recruiting and training of sales personnel; maintenance, repair, and customer service operations; and, above all, distribution and retail. For example, Midway, a marketing firm based in the People's Republic of China, has specialized in the sales and distribution functions of the children's market and has become the local licensee and distributor of choice, representing a range of firms and brands including Disney, Benetton, Mattel, Elle, and Sesame Street.[9] These multinationals have realized that Midway's ability to achieve quality distribution and merchandising in China's dominant department stores is second to none, and although they would normally prefer to have different local representatives to mitigate

---

9. David J. Arnold, "Midway: Licensing, Distributing, and Building Brands in China," Harvard Business School case study 9-02-032. Boston: Harvard Business School Publishing.

any conflicts of interest among competitive brands, they are concentrating their Chinese market penetration efforts in this sector on Midway. As discussed earlier in this book, distribution is most often the enabling condition for development of a large consumer market, and its low degree of development explains why many emerging markets are "emerging." Interestingly, distribution has been one of the last sectors to internationalize, especially retail, since it is asset intensive and embedded in a complex local supply chain.

THE ECONOMIC STRUCTURE OF SERVICE BUSINESSES— LOCALIZATION YIELDS HIGHER RETURNS

Most service businesses have different economic structures from manufacturing firms, in particular with regard to possible economies of scale. In general, service businesses have lower fixed costs (in R&D or in the set-up of a production plant, for example). In fact, the main cost drivers in many service businesses are related to individual customer accounts in the form of customer identification, selling costs, and service costs. As a consequence, these service companies are more likely to benefit from economies of scope than economies of scale. In other words, service businesses benefit more from selling a wider range of services through a single asset, such as a customer relationship or a retail outlet, than they do from achieving greater output volumes of the same product. This encapsulates the service or distributor mental model of business, which strives for greater "share of wallet" in the customer relationship rather than emphasizing expansion of the customer base for the same product. To the extent that this is true of a particular business, it has important implications for international marketing. In particular, if scale economies are at the level of an individual customer account, this means that localization will yield greater returns than in a manufacturing business. Consider an international delivery organization, such as DHL, which subcontracts space from a number of third-party airline operators rather than relying entirely on its own fleet.[10] Perhaps the most important level at which this company can achieve scale economies is at the level of the individual collection or delivery point—if multiple packages can be handled, instead of one, it transforms the economics of the transaction. Therefore, the company needs to structure incentives and control systems to encourage this, which means delegating pricing, promotion, and service design to the local level in order to adapt to a customer's work flows and so facilitate bundling of packages. Many service businesses have this economic structure, and so they would benefit from localization of marketing to a greater extent than production-oriented companies.

SUMMARY

The central tension of international marketing, between global scale and local responsiveness, is often manifested in organizational tensions. It is here that the right managerial processes can leverage the advantage of the multinational and bring global scale and knowledge to bear into markets. Some important issues encountered in this chapter include the following:

- It is at least difficult, and perhaps impossible in some cases, to map organizational structure onto organizational processes in international operations because of the greatly increased complexity of the multimarket situation. Increasingly, therefore, best practice involves establishing a structure that is loose or flexible enough to allow a variety of different processes or relationships. So, for example, one national unit may act purely as an executive agent for implementation of corporate strategy, another may act as a production hub for a whole region, and another may lead the world in new marketing ideas or product innovation.

10. Greg Conley and John A. Quelch, "DHL Worldwide Express," Harvard Business School case study 9-593-011. Boston: Harvard Business School Publishing.

- It is important to allow for "bottom-up" processes as well as the more traditional downward delegation if a multinational is to exploit the potential gains from global market participation. Only by doing so can the firm leverage the operating knowledge and market learning it derives from its internationalism, which will enable it to "think globally."

- A network organization, consisting of a linked web of diversified units with differentiated roles, is the most suitable design principle for a global marketing organization because it reflects the complexity of the global market environment and allows the organization to adapt and respond more quickly. It is a difficult managerial challenge to allow such centrifugal power to underpin an organization rather than to adopt the more traditional "head-and-body" design in which the corporate center has controlling authority and greater knowledge of the business. In particular, it is wise to retain a clearly identified leadership role for each market, segment, or product category, even though it may be in a different place for each business unit.

- The concept of a center of gravity is useful in thinking about international marketing organizations. It captures the important notion that different markets will be differently structured and that the structure may change regularly and rapidly. This will help the market-facing parts of the organization adapt more closely to the complex international markets in which it operates.

A small number of born global firms appear to bypass the traditional incremental internationalization process. In most cases, such firms build international organizations rapidly by leveraging as far as possible the networks of major clients and partners, retaining only their core asset (such as an innovative product or technology) under their own management. This new approach to building international marketing networks is only possible after considerable globalization by the larger networks to which born global firms attach. Over the long run, born global companies are likely to become more like these larger multinationals as they grow themselves, and they will encounter many of the same challenges described in the body of this book.

Service organizations can internationalize more rapidly, and respond more flexibly to changing demand conditions and market structures because of their freedom from the capital- and location-intensive assets of manufacturing businesses. Against these advantages, it is of course harder for service organizations to build the competitive barriers that can accrue from commitments to those assets. Interestingly, for many service businesses, economies of scale can only be achieved at the local level, often at the level of the individual customer: this gives service businesses a natural advantage in localization. In many cases, the challenge facing service companies is not to remain local at all points in their global network, but to achieve genuine global leverage in terms of knowledge and operations. This contrasts with manufacturing businesses, which are pushed towards global scale and consistency by their manufacturing operations and strive to remain local in all markets.

8 THE BIG IDEAS OF INTERNATIONAL MARKETING

While this book has been structured around issues facing executives in international marketing, there are a number of recurring themes underpinning a range of situations. These ideas represent some of the intellectual structure of international marketing over and above that of single market or regular marketing. They demonstrate the fact that international marketing is broader than marketing as it is usually defined— because marketing is often the dominant activity of an international firm in a foreign market, with many other functions served from other countries or regional or global centers. By contrast, in a single domestic market, a firm's full range of functions will be conducted. Thus, for example, the first of these issues, the distinction between market knowledge and marketing knowledge, would not be seen as a concept of major importance in mainstream marketing thinking because knowledge management would be regarded as a general management rather than as a marketing management issue.

The following are the fundamental issues that confront managers in international markets and explain many of the decisions taken in those markets.

MARKET KNOWLEDGE AND MARKETING KNOWLEDGE

There is an important distinction to be drawn between two types of knowledge, assumptions about which lie behind many international marketing decisions. Market knowledge can be defined as the capability required to operate a successful business in a given country or region. This may encompass a variety of facets, but it will almost certainly encompass a familiarity with local business regulations, an understanding of local culture and language, and a network of local contacts including both customers and facilitators who can be called upon to lobby on behalf of the business. This body of knowledge, which could also be described as local operating capability, is often allied with local assets such as an office, a distribution network, a workforce, and perhaps production facilities.

This is quite different from marketing knowledge. This is related to a technology or product category rather than to a geographic market, and it can be defined as the capability required to maximize sales of a given product. Marketing knowledge will almost invariably be associated with corporations that design and manufacture in the product category, and it accrues from these functions as well as from experience of commercialization in multiple markets. Thus, Henkel may be regarded as the most knowledgeable company in the world when it comes to marketing industrial adhesives, Gillette when it comes to shaving products, Boeing and Airbus when it comes to commercial aircraft, and so on.

In very many cases, these two types of knowledge are located in different organizations. Thus, for example, when contemplating entry into a smaller Latin American market it can be safely assumed that Sony will have far more expertise than any local company with regard to the marketing of consumer electronics, how to position them to highlight the key benefits, how to take them to market to accelerate adoption, and so on. But it is almost certainly also true that Sony knows little about how to operate such a market. Clearly, both types of knowledge are required in order to develop the market to its potential.

Confusion between these two types of knowledge often lies behind some of the failings in international markets identified in Chapter 1. The most common mistake is to overestimate the power of market knowledge, or operating capability, and to underleverage an international company's marketing knowledge. This may happen because the international firm is concerned mainly with risk minimization and therefore participates in the market at arm's length. In addition, many countries have regulations requiring foreign entrants to partner with a local firm, from which it can easily be assumed that local operating knowledge is all that counts. In fact, as was seen in Chapter 5, most companies end up being disappointed with their local partner and increasing their investment in the market. The clear solution to this dilemma, which experienced multinationals increasingly adopt, is to commit significant resources alongside the local partner as early as possible after entry into the market.

INVESTMENTS IN COMMITMENT PRODUCE RETURNS IN CONTROL

It has been observed several times in this book that under-commitment to a foreign market can often be observed to result in lackluster performance, which the international firm then corrects by increasing its commitment. The fact that one of the dominant models of internationalization is called the "increasing commitment" supports the argument that companies are often too slow to commit resources. It is clear, and to some extent understandable, why internationalizing companies behave in this manner—namely a concern with risk minimization. This, however, is a financial rather than a marketing perspective, and often, therefore, it unsurprisingly produces performance that is financially prudent but is an underperformance relative to market potential. The fundamental issue here is that foreign market entry and development is a high-risk situation—the uncertainty of fundamentally different market and demand structure combined with managerial unfamiliarity, make this inevitable. For a company to adopt a risk minimization strategy may be prudent from the financial perspective—if it is assumed that the decision has already been taken to enter the market. But it is worth asking whether market entry should be undertaken at all if the company is not going to commit fully to the investments it judges necessary to capture the targeted revenues and profit. A mentality of "let's test the market and see how it goes" is fundamentally flawed because the results are certain to be different from what would be achieved if full investment were made (i.e., the test does not replicate the full market scenario and does not therefore provide insight into likely future developments). There is a noticeable trend among more sophisticated and experienced multinationals to shift forward investment to market entry and immediately afterwards in an attempt to bypass the traditional long period of slow growth after market entry.

THE BEST MARKET ENTRY STRATEGY IS NOT NECESSARILY THE BEST STRATEGY FOR MARKET DEVELOPMENT

Since one of the distinguishing characteristics of international marketing is a context of rapid business growth, it is not surprising that the challenge facing any business can alter rapidly. This insight is behind some of the most influential frameworks for international marketing, such as the Douglas and Craig model described in Chapter 3. Despite this, many companies react too slowly to market development and stick too long with the strategy adopted for market entry. The strategy adopted for market entry may apply to choice of partner, product range, level of marketing expenditure allocated to sales force or advertising and promotion, or any other element of the marketing mix. In particular, it should be noted that many companies choose what might be described as the easiest strategy options at market entry—for example, targeting the "early adopters," that small group of customers most likely to adopt the new product offering—and use these options as the basis for partner selection or product positioning. However, there is often a step change required in order to penetrate the next group of customers—in this regard, development of an international market is similar to the challenge of getting an innovative product adopted in a single market. The difference is that many companies are under-committed to international markets, and they therefore display too much patience in the vain hope that time alone will result in market growth. A well-structured plan for international market development should anticipate the need for a sequenced adjustment of any element of marketing mix—the pace of market development is not predetermined.

SCALE DEMANDS CONTROL, BUT NOT STANDARDIZATION

Best practice management of many marketing mix decisions in international markets amounts to combining a core platform with locally varying elements. Thus, a brand name and visual identity may be standardized (the brand platform), but local promotion may include market-specific elements. Similarly, corporate centers may invest in promotional platforms, such as MasterCard's World Cup sponsorship, but they offer local units a range of options for execution of this central theme. Even the notion of price corridors is conceptually the same (a centrally designed constraint that allows local variation so long as that constraint is respected).

The fundamental idea behind this is closely related to the notion "think globally, act locally." But two key refinements need to be made to understand fully how this axiomatically desirable state can be reached. First, a company must understand the hierarchy of global and local elements. In other words, what is sought is not the coexistence of global and local elements in some haphazard or politically produced pattern, but clear relationships and processes linking the global and the local from each perspective. Applied to branding, for example, this means that those elements of a brand that stimulate recognition (logo, color, and other format elements) should apply everywhere because there are returns to scale in design and execution and because there are no constraints from local culture. In this sense, they should be given priority and made into rules that all national units have to follow. If this standardization were applied to those elements of the brand that stimulate interpretation and meaning, however, there would be diseconomies of scale, since those consumer processes are culture bound and vary by country or region. So, those elements should be delegated to local decision, but only so long as the global priority standards are met first.

Second, it should be understood that control can be exercised without full decision powers, just as scale can be achieved in some aspects of branding, but diseconomies can be achieved as well. The best approach, therefore, is for the global center to invest in platforms and allow local units to reap the benefits of this (i.e., the center pays). This notion of central investment and local returns, described in the account of MasterCard's sponsorship model in Chapter 4, breaks the normally valid rule that investment risk and resultant return should be co-located with the same party, but it is justified in the exceptional circumstances of international marketing and represents a way in which both the center and the local unit can achieve their respective goals.

THE STAGE OF A COUNTRY'S ECONOMIC DEVELOPMENT NEED NOT CORRELATE WITH PRODUCT-MARKET DEVELOPMENT

This point, well illustrated in the case study of the Saudi Arabian ice cream market described in Chapter 3, is related to the previous issue, since an overreliance on country-level data, which is inevitably economic in nature, can disguise substantial differences in product-market development. In the case of Saudi Arabia, there are a number of cultural factors that result in per capita consumption of ice cream being well below that in countries of comparable levels of economic development. While this results in overestimation of market potential on the part of multinationals, the opposite result is just as common: in such a case, there can be a resignation by management that market potential can only be realized at the pace of overall economic development, when in fact certain product categories may benefit from more thoughtful and perhaps aggressive investment. This may lie behind the slow business growth experienced in emerging markets by some major western multinationals (especially since those examples of rapid penetration involve just such major targeted investment) such as Procter & Gamble in Eastern Europe, Mercedes in China, or Coca-Cola in the Middle East.

PRODUCT-MARKET DATA EXPLAINS MORE THAN COUNTRY-MARKET DATA

The fact that product-market data explains more than country-market data is clearly related to the previous idea, and it is self-evidently true to any experienced international marketing executive, but the point needs highlighting simply because it is so often ignored, especially by young or inexperienced companies. Country-level data, usually concerned with macroeconomics or demographics, is the best vehicle for analysis of a country. On a conceptual level, it should be clear that it will be a blunt instrument for analysis of commercial marketing issues once the importance of market drivers and enabling conditions are understood (see Chapter 2). On an empirical level, there is ample evidence to support the argument that the same country displays highly divergent levels of attraction and risk for different companies, even different companies in the same industry with different strategies and capabilities.

CONCLUSION—INTERNATIONAL MARKETING MANAGEMENT, NOT INTERNATIONAL MARKETING

The central thesis of this book has been that while companies are globalizing, markets are localizing. A different way of expressing this argument is to say that marketing fundamentals always apply. Among the most fundamental principles of marketing are first, the importance of getting as close as possible to a market or customer group in order to discover exactly what it wants and, second, to react to this information by giving it what it wants. Many of the common pitfalls of international marketing described in this book are, in essence, symptoms of a drive to shape markets rather than the listening, reactive approach demanded by these marketing fundamentals. Just as economic fundamentals can be forgotten during speculative booms, so marketing fundamentals can be forgotten during periods of rapid corporate globalization. In both cases, however, fundamentals reassert their validity in time: as discussed in the first chapter of this book, there is already gathering evidence that markets are fragmenting, that industries are on average growing less concentrated, and that customers are as frequently sticking to established favorite brands as they are switching to global brands. Over the long run, those companies that participate in markets by listening and reacting at as local a level as possible will emerge the winners. Ironically, most multinational corporations are making significant efforts in this direction in their established markets while often simultaneously attempting, in effect, to bulldoze international markets into a single global template through replication strategies.

The mirage of global markets is produced by the very real phenomenon of globalizing companies. There are certainly valuable advantages to a global presence in several aspects of business operations, and it is impossible to imagine a reversal in the trend of corporate globalization. What is starting to become clear to the more sophisticated multinationals, however, is that the marketing advantage that accrues from being global is the power to do different things everywhere rather than the power to do the same thing everywhere. Replication strategies achieve, at best, scale—a questionable achievement in the eyes of many consumers, who are reasonably focused only on their own local needs and wants. By contrast, the learning and marketing expertise that come from a diverse portfolio of local marketing programs confer qualities essential to marketing success—knowledge, experience, and agility and flexibility in implementation. Corporations able to transfer ideas from one market to another (while simultaneously tailoring the execution to local conditions) will gain managerial advantages from being global while still playing according to marketing fundamentals. This is what it means to "think globally, act locally"—international marketing management, but local marketing.

Index

8 reasons why you should read the Financial Times for 4 weeks RISK-FREE!

To help you stay current with significant
developments in the world economy ...
and to assist you to make informed business
decisions — the Financial Times brings you:

❶ Fast, meaningful overviews of international affairs ... plus daily briefings on major world news.

❷ Perceptive coverage of economic, business, financial and political developments with special focus on emerging markets.

❸ More international business news than any other publication.

❹ Sophisticated financial analysis and commentary on world market activity plus stock quotes from over 30 countries.

❺ Reports on international companies and a section on global investing.

❻ Specialized pages on management, marketing, advertising and technological innovations from all parts of the world.

❼ Highly valued single-topic special reports (over 200 annually) on countries, industries, investment opportunities, technology and more.

❽ The Saturday Weekend FT section — a globetrotter's guide to leisure-time activities around the world: the arts, fine dining, travel, sports and more.

FT FINANCIAL TIMES
World business newspaper

The *Financial Times* delivers
a world of business news.

Use the Risk-Free Trial Voucher below!

To stay ahead in today's business world you need to be well-informed on a daily basis. And not just on the national level. You need a news source that closely monitors the entire world of business, and then delivers it in a concise, quick-read format.

With the *Financial Times* you get the major stories from every region of the world. Reports found nowhere else. You get business, management, politics, economics, technology and more.

Now you can try the *Financial Times* for 4 weeks, absolutely risk free. And better yet, if you wish to continue receiving the *Financial Times* you'll get great savings off the regular subscription rate. Just use the voucher below.

4 Week Risk-Free Trial Voucher

Yes! Please send me the *Financial Times* for 4 weeks (Monday through Saturday) Risk-Free, and details of special subscription rates in my country.

Name _____

Company _____

Address _____ ❑ Business or ❑ Home Address

Apt./Suite/Floor _____ City _____ State/Province _____

Zip/Postal Code_____ Country _____

Phone (optional) _____ E-mail (optional)_____

Limited time offer good for new subscribers in FT delivery areas only.

To order contact Financial Times Customer Service in your area (mention offer SAB01A).

The Americas: Tel 800-628-8088 Fax 845-566-8220 E-mail: uscirculation@ft.com

Europe: Tel 44 20 7873 4200 Fax 44 20 7873 3428 E-mail: fte.subs@ft.com

Japan: Tel 0120 341-468 Fax 0120 593-146 E-mail: circulation.fttokyo@ft.com

Korea: E-mail: sungho.yang@ft.com

S.E. Asia: Tel 852 2905 5555 Fax 852 2905 5590 E-mail: subseasia@ft.com

www.ft.com

FT FINANCIAL TIMES
World business newspaper

Where to find tomorrow's best business and technology ideas. TODAY.

- Ideas for defining tomorrow's competitive strategies — and executing them.

- Ideas that reflect a profound understanding of today's global business realities.

- Ideas that will help you achieve unprecedented customer and enterprise value.

- Ideas that illuminate the powerful new connections between business and technology.

ONE PUBLISHER.
Financial Times
Prentice Hall.

WORLD BUSINESS PUBLISHER

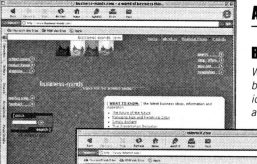

AND 3 GREAT WEB SITES:

Business-minds.com

Where the thought leaders of the business world gather to share key ideas, techniques, resources — and inspiration.

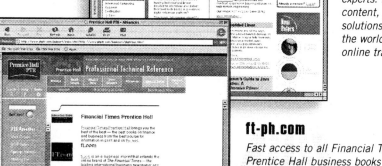

Informlt.com

Your link to today's top business and technology experts: new content, practical solutions, and the world's best online training.

ft-ph.com

Fast access to all Financial Times Prentice Hall business books currently available.